THE COMPLETE
NAPKIN BOOK

THE COMPLETE
NAPKIN BOOK

40 PRACTICAL PROJECTS AND ADDITIONAL IDEAS FOR NAPKINS, WITH BEAUTIFUL DESIGNS AND
IMAGINATIVE EMBELLISHMENTS SHOWN IN OVER 300 STUNNING COLOUR PHOTOGRAPHS

Andrea Spencer

southwater

This edition is published by Southwater, an imprint of Anness Publishing Ltd, Hermes House, 88–89 Blackfriars Road, London SE1 8HA; tel. 020 7401 2077; fax 020 7633 9499

www.southwaterbooks.com; www.annesspublishing.com

If you like the images in this book and would like to investigate using them for publishing, promotions or advertising, please visit our website www.practicalpictures.com for more information.

UK agent: The Manning Partnership Ltd;
  tel. 01225 478444; fax 01225 478440;
  sales@manning-partnership.co.uk
UK distributor: Grantham Book Services Ltd;
  tel. 01476 541080; fax 01476 541061;
  orders@gbs.tbs-ltd.co.uk
North American agent/distributor:
  National Book Network; tel. 301 459 3366;
  fax 301 429 5746; www.nbnbooks.com
Australian agent/distributor: Pan Macmillan Australia;
  tel. 1300 135 113; fax 1300 135 103;
  customer.service@macmillan.com.au
New Zealand agent/distributor: David Bateman Ltd;
  tel. (09) 415 7664; fax (09) 415 8892

Publisher: Joanna Lorenz
Editorial Director: Helen Sudell
Executive Editor: Joanne Rippin
Editor: Simona Hill
Designer: Lisa Tai
Photography: Spike Powell
Styling: Andrea Spencer
Additional Photographs and Styling: Mark Wood and Helen Trent. Nicki Dowey 44bl, 45bl (maker Susie Stokoe). Paul Bricknell 55. Debbie Patterson and Tessa Evelegh 7, 20, 21, 35tr, 37br, 43, 77. Michelle Garrett 15b, 63 (maker Dorothy Wood), 71, with Tessa Evelegh 78, with Gilly Love 36tr, 36br, with Alison Jenkins 47, and Karin Hossack 71, with Stewart and Sally Walton 45tr and 70. Polly Wreford and Tessa Evelegh 18, 19, 38, 41bl, 41br, 44tl, 45tc, 59, 61, 64, 66t, 66b, 76, 87, 90. Caroline Arber and Charlotte Melling 15. Frank Adam and Craig Robertson 32tl, 32bl, 32br.

ETHICAL TRADING POLICY

At Anness Publishing we believe that business should be conducted in an ethical and ecologically sustainable way, with respect for the environment and a proper regard to the replacement of the natural resources we employ.

As a publisher, we use a lot of wood pulp to make high-quality paper for printing, and that wood comes from spruce trees. We are therefore currently growing more than 500,000 trees in two Scottish forest plantations near Aberdeen – Berrymoss (130 hectares/320 acres) and West Touxhill (125 hectares/305 acres). The forests we manage contain twice the number of trees employed each year in paper-making for our books.

Because of this ongoing ecological investment programme, you, as our customer, can have the pleasure and reassurance of knowing that a tree is being cultivated on your behalf to naturally replace the materials used to make the book you are holding.

Our forestry programme is run in accordance with the UK Woodland Assurance Scheme (UKWAS) and will be certified by the internationally recognized Forest Stewardship Council (FSC). The FSC is a non-government organization dedicated to promoting responsible management of the world's forests. Certification ensures forests are managed in an environmentally sustainable and socially responsible way. For further information about this scheme, go to www.annesspublishing.com/trees

© Anness Publishing Ltd 2008

A CIP catalogue record for this book is available from the British Library.

Previously published as part of a larger volume, *The Complete Illustrated Book of Napkins and Napkin Folding*

Contents

Introduction

Whether you are preparing a formal feast or a simple lunch, the table sets the scene for the meal, and a beautifully and elegantly laid table creates a sense of anticipation among your guests, who can look forward to a special time together. Every table setting combines items that you use repeatedly, such as plates and glasses, with more transient elements such as flowers that give each meal a unique atmosphere. As you plan your design you'll want to take lots of things into account – the time of day, the formality of the meal, the décor of the room, and even the food you will be serving – and it's the decorative details that play a huge role in making your table look beautiful and right.

You really can create completely different looks and moods simply by changing the accessories. A table dressed for dinner in crisp white linen and your best china, then accessorized with sparkling cut glass, flickering candles and inventively folded napkins, immediately sets a formal mood for a special occasion, perhaps an important

Above White and silver, or white and gold, make a classic and elegant combination. These napkin rings when used with bright colours will also instantly adapt to a contemporary look.

celebration. For a different kind of meal you might simply replace starched white napkins with extrovert lime green ones, folded at each place or tucked into brightly coloured napkin rings, and guests will immediately anticipate an altogether more informal and relaxed affair.

The key is to invest in classic pieces of china, glass and cutlery that you know you will continue to enjoy using for years to come. These pieces will be the basic ingredients for your table settings, and you can dress them up or down to create the right ambience for each occasion. Candles and flowers, with their natural seasonal variety, have always been a quick way to make a change, but of all the other elements of table setting the easiest and most cost effective to change or adapt are the linens.

You can't go wrong by investing in exquisite white or cream dinner napkins in linen or cotton

Left Royal blue napkins and gold tableware are a perfect combination for a formal outdoor occasion. When used together these colours suggest formality and luxury.

Above A rosebud is both a simple and extravagant way to add a finishing touch to a table setting. Held in place with a delicate ribbon, this final flourish adds to the occasion. Team with old-fashioned plates and good quality neutral fabric napkins.

Right Red is the perfect colour for a festive table setting. Co-ordinating crackers decorated with gold complement the china plate perfectly.

damask. Really good quality table linens last a lifetime – or more, as they can be handed down from one generation to the next. Freshly laundered, they always look wonderful, and years of hot washing and starching give linens and heavy cottons an appearance and feel that goes on improving with age. You may have been given a set of fine linen napkins as a marvellous present, or you could scour antique markets and pick up some Victorian originals that still have plenty of life in them. They look wonderful on the table, just pressed and folded simply, but they can also be decorated to suit different events with ribbon ties, coloured napkin rings or flowers from the garden.

For a formal occasion, you can experiment with one of the more elaborate classic napkin folds.

You could pick up a few sets of napkins in bright, contemporary colours and designs from fashionable interiors stores. For less than the cost of a vase of flowers you can buy a set of napkins that will instantly change the look of your table. You can transform the look of the table further by changing the way you fold the napkins or by adding some simple decoration.

Packed into this book is a host of creative ways to use napkins in a wide range of settings and for every occasion, from weddings to picnics. You can discover novel ways to knot, wrap, embroider and decorate them, as well as making original napkin rings out of all kinds of materials. These lovely, inspirational ideas will transform the way you use napkins and add a fresh dimension to your meals.

The world of napery

Napkins have been used at the table since medieval times, and this chapter sets the scene for the feast of napkin ideas that follow. Here you will find infomation on the use and etiquette of napkins, as well as hints and tips on building a napkin collection, laundering and storing them.

Napkins through history

There's something so deeply satisfying about the look and feel of crisp, freshly laundered white linen that it has endured internationally as the most popular table covering for hundreds of years. Shaking a clean white tablecloth and letting it float down over the table is almost a ritual in many households; it's the formal beginning of every feast, whether it is an intimate family meal or a state banquet.

The individual element of table linen is the napkin. One is provided for each diner, to protect their clothes from spills and stains, to protect their hands when holding hot dishes and plates, and to dab lips and greasy fingertips. In fact, these are all functions for which the tablecloth itself was once used, and the word "napkin" comes directly from nappe, the French word for a tablecloth.

Saving the tablecloth

Napkins were unheard of in Europe until the Middle Ages, by which time there was clearly a desperate need for them. Cutlery was not widely used and people ate mostly with their hands,

which they then wiped clean on a part of the tablecloth. As each part of the meal was finished a messy debris of food built up and the cloth had to be changed, a rather disruptive procedure that held up the progress of the meal and interrupted the conversation of the diners. The French developed the idea of adding an extra cover to the edge of the table. This was easier to remove, so it could be quickly exchanged for a clean one during the meal without having to clear the rest of the table. The term "cover" is still used in restaurants today to indicate the number of diners at a table. It was not long before these covers became detached from the table and were being used as napkins in the way we know today.

Napkin fashion

By the beginning of the 17th century elaborate neck ruffs were in fashion and needed protection from spills. Instead of being laid on people's knees, napkins began to be tied around their necks, becoming ever more generously sized as the ruffs became more flamboyant. The fashion conscious and the wealthy needed the largest napkins to ensure that their ostentatious neckwear was kept stain-free.

Guests became responsible for their own napkins, choosing them to suit the size of their ruffs. Naturally, the larger the ruff the larger the napkin had to be, and over time enormous napkins became an unlikely status symbol. As fashion changed and ruffs disappeared, giving

Left *Historically cutlery, glassware and china have always been set according to a formal pattern, which ensured that the meal was served with little hindrance to diners and servers.*

way to subtler collars, hosts resumed the responsibility of providing napkins, but they lost none of their status in the process.

By the end of the 17th century, it was not just size that mattered; shape was also important. Napkins were folded into ever more ornate shapes. Fans, flowers, birds and even heraldic devices graced the smartest tables. There were special folds for gentlemen and more elaborate folds for ladies. At really smart functions, each place was given its own individual fold. The competition between hosts became so intense that London butlers were sent to Paris to learn the latest styles and perfect their folding skills.

In the elegant Georgian period fashions became much more restrained and the elaborate folding of napkins fell out of favour, as it was considered far too fussy. It was not until the mid-19th century, with the rise of the middle classes, that the fashion was resurrected, as people sought to achieve new heights of gentility. But by the end of the Victorian era, fancy folding was again regarded as a little vulgar – as was the

custom of putting napkins on side plates, which was considered to mean that the host was showing off the fine china of the main plates. Nevertheless, the classic folds have survived and can still be used to great effect to give an air of elegance and style to formally dressed tables, worthy of the grandest occasions.

Above *Dressing the table for even the simplest occasion suggests a certain formality about dining, presentation of food and expected codes of behaviour.*

Left *A picnic is a social occasion at which a napkin is an essential item.*

Napkin etiquette

The first rule with napkins is that they should be provided: as the host it is your responsibility to see that each of your guests is equipped with a freshly laundered napkin to protect their clothes and wipe their fingers. Etiquette decrees that there are napkins to suit different types of occasion and event.

What to use when

Afternoon tea, a popular meal through the 19th and 20th centuries and still a delightful way to entertain today, is the occasion on which the smallest and prettiest napkins should be brought out. Because it is seen mainly as a ladies' or children's occasion, napkins for afternoon tea have traditionally been made of delicate materials, such as fine lawn, exquisitely embroidered and measuring a tiny 20–30cm/ 8–12in square.

For the cocktail hour, which became popular early in the 20th century, small napkins made of gossamer fabrics such as lace, organza and fine cotton lawn became popular as the kind to hand out to catch drips from glasses and wipe fingers clean as the canapés were passed around. While such conventions need no longer be followed, they can add to the sense of occasion and help to set the party mood.

The general rule for napkins is: the less formal the occasion, the smaller and more decorated the napkin can be. Dinner napkins should be generously proportioned – up to 1m/1yd square – and should be used folded in half, adequately covering the most ample lap with a double thickness of good quality fabric. For less formal dinners you can use smaller napkins, about 75cm/30in square, but no smaller than 50cm/20in square.

Below A white dinner napkin over a waiter's arm looks smart, while protecting his clothes and providing an instant cloth with which to wipe any spills.

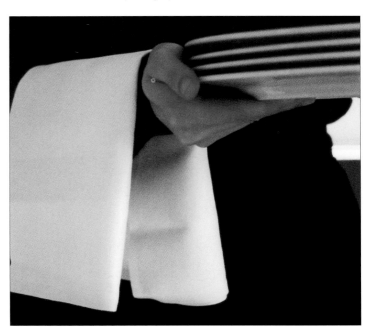

Below A napkin wrapped around the neck of a wine bottle will catch any drips as the wine is poured. It also makes holding a chilled wine or champagne bottle easier.

Right Table linen was traditionally always white. A white setting makes the table look formal and neat, while displaying many styles of tableware to its best advantage.

For most entertaining we are much more relaxed than our forebears; while white napkins remain the classic choice, patterns and colours are suitable for all but the most formal of occasions. If you keep a selection of different types, varying in size, colour and material, you are bound to be able to fit the right style to every occasion, especially if you customize them with some of the many ideas in this book.

Managing your napkin

Even today, when many of the fussier aspects of table manners have been abandoned in favour of a general awareness of the comfort of your fellow diners, there are still some formal occasions when elaborate etiquette will be observed.

At formal dinners and banquets one of the first stumbling blocks can be deciding when to unfold your napkin. In top hotels and restaurants around the world the waiters often deal with this: once everyone is seated they may go around the table, unfolding the napkins and either handing them to each guest or flicking them into their laps. If this is not done for you, wait at least until everyone is seated before unfolding your napkin, but make sure it is on your lap just as the first course arrives.

Large dinner napkins should be left folded in half, so there is a double thickness on your lap, and small napkins completely unfolded. The napkin should be left on your lap throughout the meal, except when you need to lift it to wipe your mouth. In parts of France some people still tuck their napkins into their collars, and this is perfectly proper, although in other countries at more formal occasions it may seem a little eccentric.

If, during a formal dinner, your napkin slithers off your lap, do not attempt to dive down under the table to rescue it from among other diners' feet. Attract the attention of a waiter, who will either retrieve the napkin or bring a fresh one.

When it is time to get up at the end of the meal, put your napkin on the table. In Europe it is usual to leave the napkin crumpled on the table to indicate that it is ready for laundering. In America it is more correct to leave it neatly folded. At family meals you should fold your napkin when you have finished with it, or roll it up and replace it in your napkin ring, before leaving the table, even if it needs laundering.

Using napkins

The way people eat has changed dramatically over the centuries: we may no longer spear a chicken on a knife or tear it apart with our fingers like a medieval banqueter, but nor do we feel the need to eat a banana with a knife and fork or serve lamb chops dressed with little paper frills, as was à la mode a few generations ago. However, while fashions in etiquette come and go, napkins remain a basic adjunct of our eating habits, and not only at the dinner table. Even if you're just eating a sandwich on the beach or a burger at a street party, a napkin comes in useful – though it's most likely to be a paper one.

Eating at the table

For everyday family meals, napkins are there to wipe fingers and mouths and protect everyone's clothes. Unless they get dirty during a meal they can be folded or rolled up ready for next time, and named or monogrammed napkin rings mean that everyone knows which one is theirs.

At formal meals, when your guests are dressed in their best clothes, they'll appreciate large dinner napkins that sit securely in their laps just in case of drips and spills. When you're serving

wine, wrapping a napkin round the bottle will stop condensation or iced water from a chilled bottle trickling on to your guests as you fill their glasses, or drips of red wine staining the tablecloth. Luxurious, thick napkins can be helpful when handing round hot dishes or plates, or lifting the lids of hot dishes, and you can also use their insulating properties by tucking them around a batch of hot bread rolls or tortillas. If you're serving food that is to be eaten with the fingers, it's a good idea to provide paper as well as fabric napkins, but bear in mind that the fabric ones may get quite dirty too, and replacements may be welcomed for the remainder of the meal.

When buying or making fabric napkins, it's worth bearing all these possible uses in mind, as it's clear that there are advantages to having a generous number in each set. Allow for plenty of matching spares for tasks such as wrapping bottles, lining baskets for bread or fruit, or supplying replacements if napkins get lost under the table or have to be used to mop up a spill.

Barbecues and picnics

Most outdoor eating tends to be fairly informal, but people still like to be able to wipe their fingers. Barbecue food is not only sticky but also hot, so plenty of napkins will protect fingers and clothes and can even be used as impromptu tablecloths on the grass or the beach. A roll of paper towels may be practical when you're eating outdoors (and you should certainly have

Left Napkins wrapped around hot serving dishes can be used to match the setting of the day, while protecting your hands from the heat.

Right *For serve-yourself buffet-type functions leave a pile of napkins with the plates so that guests can help themselves.*

Below *For outdoor eating individually wrap a place setting of knife, fork and spoon in its own napkin. That way the cutlery won't get lost in transit and every guest will be catered for.*

and fruit – much more picturesque and appetizing than plastic bags and boxes. A really grand picnic deserves to be eaten from proper china rather than paper plates, so use napkins to protect the crockery while travelling to the picnic spot.

On a smaller scale than the classic picnic hamper, a small basket lined with a colourful napkin can turn a simple offering of food, such as a pie for an elderly relative or some fruit from your garden for a new neighbour, into a delightful gift.

Treats on trays

Half the fun of taking someone breakfast in bed is in the setting of the tray: the best china, a flower or two, some delicious food, and of course, a pretty napkin to complete the picture – and perhaps another to line the tray. This kind of attention to detail can also help to cheer someone up when they're ill in bed or just languishing on the sofa. Even if they don't feel like eating much they'll appreciate the trouble you've taken.

one handy), but it's so much more fun to unpack a picnic hamper in which the food is excitingly hidden under bright, colourful cotton napkins. Hearty, overfilled French bread sandwiches can be individually wrapped in napkins to hold them together and contain the crumbs, and you can also use napkins to parcel up home-made cakes

Placing and presenting napkins

Crisp, freshly laundered napkins are an essential feature of every well-set table. They may be pressed in large, plain squares and laid at each place with the minimum of fuss, or folded in a variety of ways to complement the meal and the style of the table setting, using some of the ingenious ideas presented in this book.

Traditionally, a plainly folded napkin is placed in the centre of each place setting, between the knife and fork. However, if you plan to put the first course of a meal on the table before everyone is seated, the folded napkin would go to the left of the place setting, on the side plate, in which case you would probably fold it into an oblong or triangle, or roll it. A complex, sculptural fold can be placed in the centre of a dinner plate, or may be designed to occupy a bowl or a glass. Napkins can also be arranged to hold a set of cutlery, chopsticks, a place card, a flower, or even a small gift. Whatever the arrangement, make sure your assemblage is quick and easy to dismantle when the meal begins.

On a buffet table, it's best to stack napkins simply and provide a generous amount: bear in mind that guests rarely retain their napkins after the main course and many may take a second one with their dessert. Roll a napkin around each knife and fork, or pile the napkins in a basket near the plates and cutlery.

Simple presentation

If your table setting is very elaborate, with flowers at each place and spectacular china and glassware, it's often best to keep the napkin folds simple, and this is obviously appropriate for

Above *For a large buffet gathering, wrap each individual set of cutlery in its own napkin so that guests can take their own once they have served themselves from the buffet.*

informal occasions. But they should still be impeccably clean and pressed. To form a neat square, press the napkin, making sure all the corners are true. Fold it in half and then in half again, pressing each fold. It may be laid square or at a diagonal between the knife and fork. If you are using very large napkins, it may be better to fold them in thirds in each direction to make a square of the perfect size – this takes some practice.

To make a triangle, fold the square diagonally and press the fold. Lay the napkin on a side plate with the long side nearest the fork, or on a plate in the middle of the setting.

A simple oblong made by folding a square in half is an ideal way to display a napkin with a decorative or monogrammed corner. Alternatively, with plain napkins folded and pressed into quarters, opposite sides of the square may be folded underneath and pressed to make an oblong shape. Lay the short side with the hemmed edge at the bottom of the setting.

Rolled napkins, secured with rings or tied with ribbon or cord, will sit neatly in place if they are laid on the table or plate with the edge of the roll underneath.

Tips for successful folding

For the best results, use heavy linen napkins not less than 45cm/18in square. The napkins must be cut square and the fabric must be cut straight on the weave, so that it will not easily pull out of shape. Linen for folding should be washed, starched and ironed while damp. Gently pull the napkin back into shape if necessary as you iron, to ensure it is perfectly square.

Iron on a large surface – an ironing board can be too narrow when pressing large napkins. Use a table instead, protecting the surface with a thick, folded towel covered with a piece of plain white cotton. Dampen napkins that have dried before ironing. Use traditional starch (spray starch will not give a sufficiently crisp finish). Traditional starch may be mixed and sprayed on linen using a clean plant spray. Allow it to soak into the fabric for a minute or two before ironing.

When you are folding napkins into complicated shapes, press each fold individually for the best results; soft folds should not be pressed.

Below *A white table setting with matching napkins suggests formality. Shaking out the napkin is a clear signal that the meal is about to commence.*

Buying and choosing fabric

You cannot go wrong with plain white linen napkins. Freshly laundered and sweetly scented, they have been the correct choice for formal occasions since the 16th century. The finest napkins are made of silk damask – characterized by intricate designs incorporated into the weave – which was introduced into Europe from Damascus in the Middle East by returning Crusaders in the 12th century.

Once damask had arrived in Europe, textile workers in France, Flanders and Ireland learnt the weaving techniques and the designs used to make it, and applied them to linen, and later to cotton. Traditionally, a set of damask table linens embroidered with a family monogram formed part of a young woman's dowry, and damask remains the most popular choice for table napkins today.

Practical qualities

While starched white damask is perfect for the most formal meals, most entertaining today is far more relaxed. Napkins in deep colours or with all-over patterns can be used on almost any occasion, helping to create the mood and look you want for your table or party setting. But even if bright green or deep red napkins are key to the colour scheme of your table setting, don't forget that these objects are not just for looking at: napkins are first and foremost useful articles, and their tactile quality and absorbency is important.

Delicate little squares of lace or lawn make charming accessories for tea parties or cocktails, but for other occasions go for more substantial fabrics that will cope with spills and sticky fingers. Each guest will handle their napkin, even if only when laying it on their lap, so the fabric should be

Above *Damask cotton napkins with a woven pattern are hard-wearing and serviceable. These will last for years and washing will soften the woven fabric.*

Above *Antique lace-edged napkins are most likely to have been embroidered at home, and are valued for the quality of their workmanship. They can often be bought second-hand.*

a pleasure to touch. For this reason, it needs to be smooth and thick, and faultlessly pressed. Napkins of a generous size and weight not only feel better but are less likely to slip off people's knees and disappear under the table. On another practical note, it's vital to use fabric that's tough enough to stand up to rigorous washing: one good reason for the popularity of white linen and cotton is that they can be boiled or bleached to get rid of stains and give a scrupulously clean finish every time. If you are choosing coloured napkins, or fabrics for making your own, make sure they are colourfast and can be washed and ironed on hot settings.

For folding purposes, heavy linen is best, as it becomes firm and crisp when starched. Plain napkins should measure 45–50cm/18–20in square, or more, and this size is essential for many of the more complicated folds shown in this book. Otherwise, look for natural fabrics and good quality weaves that press beautifully and keep their shape. Woven stripes and checks will stay square and if you are making your own napkins the patterns act as useful guides for cutting and hemming.

Paper napkins

For large parties and informal occasions such as barbecues, paper napkins are more practical than fabric ones. Make sure they are large and fairly thick. Fold them in half then fan them out in a large basket on a buffet table, perhaps folding one napkin into a water lily shape for the centre of the arrangement. When laying a garden table, allow two or three different coloured napkins for each place setting. Fan them simply or fold a pair in contrasting colours together in a water lily or roll-top design.

Above *Good quality linen has an even weave making it perfect to decorate with drawn thread work or with a bound edging.*

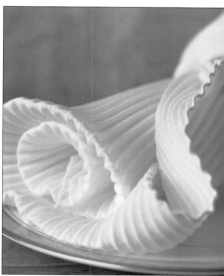

Right *Luxury fabrics add a special quality to a table setting.*

Japanese paper napkins, though fine and thin, are quite strong. They are often delicately patterned and may be round or square, with fluted or gilded edges. They can be used on their own, or in conjunction with fabric napkins if you have chosen a course for a formal meal that is eaten with the fingers. Fold them attractively with the fabric napkins; clear the paper napkins away with the plates before the next course.

Laundering and aftercare

Since the main raison d'être of table linen is to catch spills, stain removal has always been the first step in laundering. Modern proprietary stain removers followed by a machine wash have made this easier, but there are still particular stains that require a little attention.

Washing

Linen is strong, largely shrink-resistant, and can be safely washed at 60°C/140°F, which effectively washes out most food stains. Densely woven white cottons can also be washed at 60°C/140°F, though looser weaves, coloureds and polyester mixes should be laundered at no more than 40°C/100°F.

Pressing

The key to getting the best from any napkin is in the starching and pressing. A well-starched napkin holds its folds the best, and perfectionists will add traditional starch to the rinsing water.

LAUNDRY SYMBOLS

WASHING

 The number inside the wash tub symbol indicates the maximum centigrade temperature you can used using a normal wash cycle.

 A single bar below the wash tub symbol indicates a gentler washing action. This symbol is used for synthetic fabrics.

 Two bars under the wash tub symbol indicates the wool wash so a delicate cycle should be used.

 This symbol is used for hand wash garments only. The label will give other details such as temperature, drying and ironing.

 A crossed out wash tub indicates dry cleaning only.

DRY CLEANING

 A P indicates that certain solvents are suitable.

 A bar under a circle indicates the garment is sensitive to some dry cleaning processes.

 An A means that all solvents normally used for dry cleaning are suitable.

 A crossed out circle shows that the garment is not suitable for dry cleaning.

IRONING

 Three dots indicate the hottest setting on an iron.

 Two dots indicate the medium heat setting.

 The iron with one dot is used for synthetic fabrics.

 A crossed out iron means do not iron.

TUMBLE DRY

 This symbol indicates that the garment may be tumble dried.

 A single dot means the garment should be dried on the lowest heat setting.

 Two dots indicate that the garment can be dried on the high heat setting.

 A crossed out symbol means the garment is not suitable for tumble drying.

 This symbol indicates the garment should be dried flat away from direct heat.

BLEACHING

 A triangular symbol refers to chlorine bleach only.

 A crossed out triangle means do not use chlorine bleach.

Nowadays few of us have the time for traditional starching. However you can quickly achieve similar results by stretching the still damp napkins into shape, then pressing them using a little spray starch and a non-steam iron on a hot setting. Start by pressing on the reverse side to avoid any watermarks and to remove most of the creases, then on the right side, to enhance the linen's natural sheen. Re-press any napkins flat before making any of the napkin folds.

Left Drying linens over lavender bushes is an old-fashioned but easy way to add scent to your laundry. Choose a day when the linen won't blow away.

Above Linen should be stored in a clean and dry cupboard. If it is linen that is used infrequently, adding sprigs of herbs will keep it smelling fresh for the next occasion when it is used.

Storing

Linens were once stored in airing cupboards with slatted shelves to allow plenty of ventilation to the fabric and to prevent mildew and damp from occurring. They were also often scented with lavender, which is a natural antiseptic and insect repellent. Nowadays, with central heating, our houses are much drier and most of us do not have the same problems with mildew and damp, so linens can safely be kept in drawers and cupboards with solid shelves. Few of us have time to make scented lavender bags but the increasingly popular modern alternative is to use scented ironing water (there's plenty of lavender- or rose-scented water available) and then to line drawers with scented drawer liners, ensuring linens stay fresher for longer. Alternatively you could buy ready-made herb bags.

STAIN REMOVAL

Candle wax
Scrape off any excess. Sandwich the stained area between two pieces of blotting paper or brown wrapping paper, then press using a warm, dry iron. The wax will melt and be absorbed by the paper.

Red wine
There are two traditional methods of removing red wine. Treat immediately – while you are still at the table, depending on the formality of the occasion. First, soak up the spill with a kitchen towel. Then either douse the red wine with white wine and the stain should disappear, or sprinkle on a thick layer of salt, to soak up the wine.

Spicy food
This can be stubborn and often bleach may be the only answer. Start by trying a stain remover. If you are still left with a stain, soak white cloths in a bleach solution of 1 tablespoon of bleach to 1 litre (1¾ pints) of water. Launder as normal.

Scorch marks
The use of a hot iron to press napkins means they are vulnerable to scorch marks. Avoid this by ironing while still damp and by keeping the iron moving. If a napkin does become scorched, soak it in cold milk as soon as possible, or soak in a bleach solution of 1 tablespoon of bleach to 1 litre (1¾ pints) of water.

Napkins for all occasions

From ritzy cocktail parties to friendly suppers, and from formal weddings to picnics on the beach – wherever there is food or drink, napkins are needed. Here you will find ideas to match the napkin to the event.

Inspirational ideas

Whether you're using dramatic coloured linens or classic white damask, table napkins are an important part of the whole decorative scheme, adding strong colour and texture or striking a formal note. You need to plan the colour and style of your table setting as a whole, carrying a theme through and making sure it harmonizes with the room's décor, the occasion and the food.

Above Thick, crisp linen looks fabulous in strong colours that bring out its texture.

Above Hide neatly folded napkins in smart tracing paper envelopes.

Above For a celebration table, place a few elegant dragées inside each napkin.

Above Loosely tuck folded napkins into glasses to add height to the table setting.

Above For an oriental feel, tie napkins with natural string and curtain weights.

Above Enfold pre-starter nibbles in pure white napkins on each side plate.

Above *Beautiful colour-matching of accessories makes a very elegant table.*

Above *Delicately patterned china and pale linens create a period look.*

Above *A well co-ordinated green theme gives a calm, mellow look to the table.*

Above *Bend a piece of silver wire into a simple heart shape and entwine with red wool for a charming Valentine's day decoration.*

Above *Antique green plates and white table linen strike a fresh, outdoor note that is perfect for lunch on a summer's day.*

Above *The classic combination of blue and white is timeless, whatever the style.*

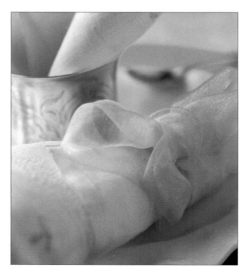

Above *Use white linens with silver and coloured filmy ribbons for a christening.*

Above *Accessorize with white daisies to complete a fresh, summery table.*

Weddings

Memorable and romantic, wedding tables have a lot to live up to. The bride needs to adore the look you create because it is, after all, her day. Yet the decorations need to appeal to guests of every generation.

Flowers will be an important part of the table decorations, and the colour scheme chosen for these can be carried through into the trimmings of napkins to give a co-ordinated look, perhaps using some of the same flowers. Many brides like to add a pretty bonbonnière or favour for each guest, and these could be tucked into each napkin as a surprise.

White napery is the safest route to follow, but this need not limit you to a traditional look. White can look equally good in a sleek minimalist setting, with the flowers and napkin ties providing accent colours.

Left Crisp white napkins are given the romantic treatment with a single deep pink rose (which sweetly matches the pattern of the traditional china) tucked into a delicate lilac organza bow.

Above Delightfully feminine and undeniably bridal, this rolled napkin has been tied with a generous organza bow. Small hedgerow flowers tucked into the fold look simple and pretty and evoke sweet-smelling summer meadows.

Above A neatly folded napkin tied with narrow ribbon makes an elegantly restrained statement. Tuck in a sprig of a fragrant herb, such as lavender or rosemary, that will not wilt during the meal.

Right Champagne, candelabras and sparkling glassware set the celebratory tone of this classic wedding table. The deep pink roses at each place setting look simple and fresh as well as being unashamedly romantic. Their strong colour is carried along the snowy white tablecloth by a seemingly artless scattering of matching petals.

Celebrate in style

Significant events such as anniversaries or naming ceremonies deserve a degree of formality that lends importance to the occasion. A good starting point is to work out a colour scheme that complements both the event and the room, and creates a sense of harmony. The style of the table setting will also depend on the age of the guest or guests of honour: for a golden wedding or eightieth birthday you will probably want to set the table in a classic style, with white napery and the family silver, whereas for an engagement party a bold, modern theme would be appropriate, and for a christening you might want to use baby pinks or blues.

Choose napkins, china and glassware that suit the occasion, picking up the tones of the furniture and décor, and accentuate your scheme with a clever choice of flowers.

Left A single pink hydrangea floret laid casually on each folded napkin adds a finishing touch that will charm guests of any age at a special family meal.

Above *Purple anemones set off the deep blue plates and tone with the lilac chair covers. For this elegant formal scheme the linen napkins have been very simply folded.*

Above *This exquisitely pretty floral theme, with the warm pink of the china matched by the ebullient hydrangea flowers, is perfectly set off by classic monogrammed damask napkins.*

Family lunch

Delicious food, simply prepared and set out on a table laid with colourful linen and earthenware crockery, sets the ambience for a warm, friendly family get-together. You'll want to keep the mood very informal for a relaxed atmosphere, but a prettily laid table will help to give the meal a sense of occasion. Whether you eat around a big kitchen table or outside in the garden, bright, homespun cotton or linen napkins provide bright accents of colour while maintaining the casual, easy-going style.

If you are hosting a buffet or barbecue, plenty of napkins are still a good idea; you can use them to mop up spills and to wipe children's sticky hands and faces.

Below *Folksy cotton tablecloths and napkins are perfect for family meals around the kitchen table, with pretty embroidered details to add charm and interest.*

Above *Take inspiration from the Mediterranean, where they know how to turn a family meal into a party. Spread a colourful, country-style cloth and add napkins in toning colours.*

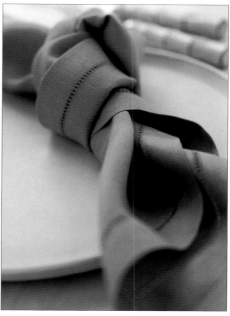

Above *Instead of folding crisp linen napkins, bring out the casual style of the meal by tying each one into a loose, chunky knot to give the table setting an impromptu look.*

Supper for friends

Entertaining nowadays is easy, informal and relaxed. Simple dishes made with delicious fresh ingredients can be quickly put together and laid out on platters for a meal that is a visual delight.

Avoid making the table setting too fussy; it doesn't matter if you don't own enough matching plates or napkins to cater for all your guests, simply mix up what you have, then pile them high for an abundant look. The key is to keep to a colour theme: all white, perhaps, so you can mix old and new. Alternatively, you could assemble shades that are tonally compatible or, on the more adventurous side, those that contrast. If you need to use china and glassware that mix a lot of different colours and patterns, you can help to create a sense of harmony on the table by choosing a linking shade in the fabric of the tablecloth and the napkins.

Above *By keeping to an all-white scheme when catering for a large number, your table will always look coordinated, however many different sets of china and napery you need to use.*

Above *Even the simplest table setting can be given a dash of contemporary style, and a seasonal accent, with the addition of a single flower from the garden.*

Left *Cottons and linens in woven stripes create a rustic mood for impromptu meals. Over the years, with repeated laundering, these traditional fabrics take on a beautiful softness.*

The cocktail hour

Recreate the pure glamour of the jazz age in your own home with an impeccably organized cocktail party, with everyone dressed in their best, a generous selection of classic cocktails, and irresistible nibbles circulating freely.

For a cocktail party to run really smoothly, you need to pay special attention to the practicalities. With everyone standing around, glass in hand, there are bound to be a few inelegant spills, so equip both your guests and the servers with suitable small-scale napkins that are as elegant as the occasion. Hark back to the heyday of the formal cocktail party with beautifully embroidered and crisply starched napkins of miniature dimensions. If you can find cocktail-sized vintage napkins with deliciously thick embroidery or Art Deco trimmings they'll really help to set the correct retro tone for the occasion.

Right *The fuss-free simplicity of these pure white linen napkins looks ultra-chic with the geometric lines of classic Martini cocktail glasses.*

Left *Guests can use small cocktail napkins under their glasses as refills are poured to catch any spills or drips.*

Above *A delicately embroidered napkin tucked into each champagne glass (with a pretty swizzle stick) strikes a lovely whimsical note for guests at a proper cocktail party.*

Afternoon tea

Tea served in the drawing room, or under a leafy tree in the garden, with fine bone china cups and saucers, thinly cut sandwiches and luscious home-made cakes, is a meal that speaks of a bygone age and a more leisurely lifestyle than most of us enjoy nowadays. However, it's fun to recreate this mood sometimes, and a charming way to entertain weekend guests.

Everything on the tea table needs to be delicately pretty, and dainty napkins with floral embroidery or lacy edgings are a must, to go with your best floral china tea service.

Above A cool green and white jacquard-woven linen napkin goes perfectly with this traditional flowered bone china tea set, arranged on a wicker tray ready for tea in the garden.

Left Delicious home-made chocolate biscuits are prettily decorated for a special tea and presented on a faultlessly starched linen napkin.

Above *Delicate crystallized rose petals are the romantic finishing touch on these lovely home-made biscuits for a special tea, and their pretty colour is echoed in the pink and white napkins.*

Above *In a more contemporary take on the traditional floral theme, this funky striped china is accompanied by napkins in a bold printed cotton with large-scale flowers.*

A summer picnic

Arrange a memorable summer outing with friends and family by packing a picnic to take to a glorious secluded corner of the countryside, or simply carry your meal out into the garden. Dainty, floral-patterned cotton table linen evokes summer meadows and will happily mix and match with striped cloths in similar tones.

Your delicious picnic fare will be even more enticing and appetizing if you pack it into a traditional wicker hamper. Include a colourful tablecloth to spread on the grass for your feast, and use co-ordinating napkins to wrap loaves, home-made pies and fruit.

Above *Stuff crusty baguettes with tempting fillings and wrap each in a colourful napkin to keep them fresh and make them easy to hold at your picnic.*

Above *A brightly striped tablecloth teamed with pretty floral napkins sets the scene for a picnic lunch in the garden. A jugful of summer flowers turns it into a special occasion.*

Above *Load the car with a colourful rug and a groaning hamper, with delicious food wrapped in colourful napkins, and set off for a perfect summer picnic in the countryside.*

A beach party

Sea air can be guaranteed to give everyone a hearty appetite, the perfect excuse for lunch at the beach. You can put up a beach umbrella and spread your picnic rug on the sand, but a long, lazy lunch can be so much more pleasurable when set up on a trestle table with some folding chairs away from the crowds. Set it with plain napkins and unbreakable enamelware, and choose seaside shades of blues and aquas teamed with plenty of white to keep the look fresh. Even on the warmest, sunniest days, you'll need to go prepared to cope with the elements: linens need to be anchored down on breezy beaches, so before you set the table scour the shore for attractive pebbles to keep each napkin decoratively in its place.

Right *For a delightfully simple lunch on the beach, put your picnic in a sturdy hamper and eat it while on the sand or in a deckchair. Lining the basket with a colourful cotton napkin will help to keep the sand out of your food.*

Above *A blue and white colour scheme is always successful at the seaside: stripes and checks look clean and fresh and go perfectly with enamel plates and sun-bleached paintwork.*

Above *If you put each filled baguette in a different colour napkin there's no arguing about which is whose – so children can nibble their lunch before rushing off, then come back for more later on.*

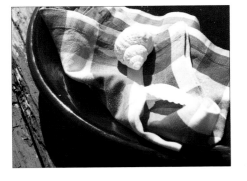

Left *Tablecloths and napkins will need anchoring to stop them being blown around by a stiff sea breeze.*

Outdoor living

When summer comes the garden can be turned into an outdoor room, and every meal of the day can be eaten at the garden table in a relaxed and less formal manner. There's no reason why it shouldn't be as attractive as your table indoors, with a jug of flowers, tablecloths and napkins, pretty crockery and glassware, and candles in the evening.

Choose table linens in bright fresh colours that will look good in bright sunlight, or in the cool green shade of a leafy tree, and easy cotton fabrics like seersucker patterned with gingham. If your garden furniture is painted, seek out napkins and crockery that suit its colour scheme to create an idyllic garden picture that will give you pleasure on every warm day of the year.

Right *When the garden is full of flowers in the summer, don't forget to pick some to decorate the table. These deep purple geraniums look wonderful with blue napkins and plates.*

Above *White place mats and neatly folded white napkins, with elegant plates and glassware, can create an effective setting for a formal meal on the garden terrace.*

Above *Even if you're not going out for a picnic, you can create a lunch to remember by packing a basket with fresh food and lemonade and carrying it to the bottom of the garden.*

Festive occasions

Buying special Christmas tableware can be an extravagance that proves too costly for the time of year. Plan, instead, to add festive touches with napkins and accessories that add the glamour and glitter. This is the time of the year when you can go over the top with gold and silver to bring sparkle to the festivities.

While you're unlikely to own a whole dinner service that is specially decorated for Christmas, it can be a joy to collect a few items of tableware that are unpacked at this one time of year – a glass dessert dish sprinkled with gold stars, or a

cake stand wreathed with holly. A set of beautiful linen napkins embroidered with Christmas motifs would be a pleasure to make and could become a well-loved feature on your festive table, one of your family's Christmas traditions.

Left Deep, rich colours with some added sparkle conjure up the spirit of Christmas as a time of light and warmth in a cold, dark season.

Left Ties of golden cord with tasselled ends lend an elegant touch of classic Christmas glamour to a set of antique monogrammed damask napkins.

Above A pure white table setting is a wonderfully delicate festive touch with a simple ivy leaf decoration at each place and a collection of sparkling Venetian coloured glasses.

Above A gold and white scheme, with touches of traditional Christmas greenery, allows you to create a table with plenty of glamour and sparkle without going over the top.

Easter

A party table for an Easter meal is the perfect setting for a celebration of the beginning of a new season after the long, dark winter months. As the sunlight strengthens, your table can reflect the freshness of the outdoor scene with clear greens, pinks and yellows. An artlessly arranged mixture of bright daffodils, tulips and hyacinths – perhaps brought straight in from the garden – will bring the scent of spring into the room and make a beautiful Easter centrepiece with a pretty basket of traditionally decorated eggs.

Choose napkins for your Easter table in pretty flower colours, or fresh stripes or prints. Tie them with ribbons and tuck a few primroses into each knot, or fold them loosely and hide a tiny Easter treat inside, such as a foil-covered chocolate rabbit or a few speckled candy eggs.

Above right *Coloured sugar mice peeping out of cones of felt in contrasting shades make an Easter table decoration that will enchant children of all ages.*

Below *The classic colour scheme of blue and white is full of the appeal of the new season, and can be given a special twist for the Easter table with an original collection of stencilled eggs.*

Above *Nestle a little posy of spring flowers such as primulas from the garden into each napkin for seasonal appeal and a focus of fresh colour.*

Whites

Whatever the style of your décor, you can always be confident that white will work on the table. Extremely elegant, it is the darling of top chefs because it complements all types of food perfectly. At home, white table linens will prove a good investment because you can mix, match and add to your collection over the years.

If you only ever buy one set of napkins, pure white linen or double damask has to be the best choice. This may appear to be extravagant at the time, but both launder beautifully, and will retain their quality no matter how much you use them. If anything they will improve with age, and you may prefer to hunt for a set of antique linen, with neatly hand-stitched hems and embroidery.

Choose pure whites for sophistication, perhaps adding exquisitely scented flowers to the setting, or use creamy white napkins for warm elegance.

Above The elegant appearance of smooth blue-white porcelain is perfectly offset by the textural contrast provided by these elaborately pleated white napkins.

Above With an all-white setting, interesting textures come to the fore: these crisply woven drawn-threadwork napkins in off-white look gorgeous tied simply with ordinary household string.

Right The colour and style of this modern creamy-white china is perfectly matched by contemporary linens in a plain but textured weave.

Brights

For an instant change of mood on your table that will have a powerful influence on the look of the whole room, add a splash of colour. Fashion has come off the catwalk to influence interiors, and if you want to set your table with your current favourite shade, the easiest way to do it is to indulge yourself with some bright new napkins. Many high-street stores stock inexpensive cotton sets in all the latest hues, or, failing that, you could just buy a metre of fabric in the perfect colour and cut out and stitch your own napkins. They will probably cost you less than a vase of flowers, and they create instant impact.

If you have coloured china, find a perfect match or go for a strong contrast. In a neutral, minimalist, setting, you could also have fun with a multi-coloured set in hot orange, pink and red, or strong blues and yellows.

Above *Vibrant contrasting colours with touches of gold embroidery give your table setting an Indian flavour.*

Above *Mix napkin colours with confidence by picking out some of the tones in a patterned or striped tablecloth.*

Above *A glorious mixture of warm, deep colours, unified by carefully selected detailing, creates a sumptuous effect.*

Above *Traditional Provençal printed cottons, in sun-drenched colours and simple designs, give the table a bright summery feel.*

Pastels

Sweetly pretty pastel colours add a friendly touch to your table, softening and warming the severity of a white tablecloth. They are easy on the eye and a positive pleasure. Use a single colour to set a mood, or play around with a mixture of delicate shades to create a table setting with the charm of a bowl of sugared almonds.

While deep, strong colours are at their best on a candlelit dinner table, pastels are the soft fresh colours of daylight. Apple blossom pink, primrose yellow or the palest greens echo the colours of the garden and are perfectly matched with delicate flowers, whether arranged as a centrepiece or held individually with ribbons or ties on each napkin. Use pastel-coloured napkins with plain white china and fine clear glassware for the most subtle effects.

Above *Tucking pastel napkins into transparent white organza sachets adds translucency as just a hint of colour shows through, emphasized by tiny sprigs of fresh flowers.*

Above *Pale spring green looks wonderfully fresh on the table, especially when teamed with crockery in clear, glowing colours, bringing a feeling of the outdoors to the table.*

Above *Warm pink is a summery colour and a delightful foil for the fresh greens of fruits and salads, making the meal a visual delight as well as an appetizing feast.*

Neutrals

The colours of the earth, from palest bone white to dark peat brown, mix naturally together to make a harmonious whole. Used for a table setting, this tranquil palette is an appropriate backdrop for delicious meals of wholesome, organic food. Yet neutrals are completely in tune with modern interiors, and just as much at home in a chic city environment as on a rustic scrubbed kitchen table.

The soft colour variations of undyed homespun linen are a perfect match for its knobbly, crunchy texture. Set it against smooth white plates on a plain tablecloth, and accessorize neutral napkins with rings and ties of natural materials such as rough sisal string. You could edge white cotton napkins with bands of grey or brown to give your table a cool, urban look.

Above *This beautiful antique French napkin, in creamy white enhanced by a soft red stripe, has been neatly folded and fastened by cord wound around a matching pair of bone buttons.*

Above *The muted shading of natural, undyed linen is perfectly matched by trimmings drawn from the natural world: a simple wicker ring and a selection of subtly striped feathers.*

Above *An elegantly simple basketwork knot is secured by a fascinating bone tag, whose sparing decoration and smooth surface contrasts beautifully with the homespun napkin.*

Florals

No table is complete without a simple arrangement of flowers to please the eye during a meal, and flowers have always been an intrinsic and important part of table decoration. They are a time-honoured motif for embroidery and textile printing, and floral designs on tablecloths can range from the discreet, stylized patterns of white damask to bold full-blown printed roses or embroidered designs of tiny sprigs and trailing stems. Printed or painted on a tea set, floral patterns evoke a gentler age of afternoon tea taken from fine bone china cups.

Floral prints make enchanting napkins, especially when the colours are light and bright and the designs are daintily small. Team them with old-fashioned china, such as an antique flower-strewn tea set or a traditional blue and white striped breakfast service.

Right *These hydrangea florets are a perfect match for the delicate willow green of the napkin, and make an ideal flower decoration for a simple raffia tie.*

Above *Floral patterns in table linens and china can be mixed together quite happily as long as you select colours of similar tones and patterns of comparable scale.*

Left *Any flower in pink or red, picked fresh from the garden, makes a glorious table decoration in summer. Strengthen the visual effect with napkins of the same colour.*

Nature table

Work with the seasons to keep your table settings looking fresh and interesting. By taking inspiration from nature, the table will always look instinctively right, yet your decorations will often cost absolutely nothing as the raw materials are just outside your door.

The key to carrying off this effect successfully when decorating napkins is to add just the smallest sprig, or a single leaf, berry or flower to capture the essence of the natural scene, without gilding the lily. Keep your eyes open for interesting stems, pebbles, shells and feathers when you're out walking, and try to use other accessories that suit the mood of the season: tie napkins with sheer ribbons in pastel colours for spring, and bind them with sisal string or raffia in autumn to blend effectively with coloured leaves and springs of ripened berries.

Above *For a really charming summer table setting, make traditional chains of simple lawn daisies and other little flowers to dress bright napkins.*

Above *Add fallen leaves in tones of russet and orange to napkins in warm autumnal colours, and conjure up the season of mists and fruitfulness.*

Above *Add a delicate seasonal touch to a formal table design by weaving tiny sprigs of flowers into silver napkin rings around traditional damask napkins.*

Left *In winter, crisp red and white checked napkins look fabulous in a ring of woven twigs, entwined with a stem of ivy and a few red berries.*

Above *Striking leathery dark green leaves make dramatically shaped ties around pale napkins for a meal set on a shady table in the garden.*

Stripes and checks

There are fresh combinations of colours and patterns that are destined to never date. Used to decorate china, blue and white has managed to top the popularity stakes for more than 200 years since 18th-century Chinese imports inspired Josiah Spode to design the ever popular Willow Pattern. Unlikely to fall from favour now, this colourway is a useful linen cupboard mainstay, especially if you choose smart checks and stripes.

Other colours work equally well in these classic woven designs, and are easy to find whether you are buying new or antique textiles. You can build up a collection gradually, teaming windowpane weaves with smaller checks, and adding bold and narrow stripes. Don't worry if the colours are not an exact match, but bear in mind that while two different shades of the same colour could look like a mistake, three or more look planned.

Left *Fabrics with woven stripes have a very traditional character. They always look smart and neat and fit easily into any setting and any colour scheme.*

Above *Checks in different sizes mix and match beautifully. Pick up the colour of the linens in the decoration of the tableware, as in the blue rims of these traditional enamelled plates.*

Left *A single pattern, such as this classic gingham check, gives a unifying theme to a collection of napkins, enabling you to mix together as many colours as you like for an original look.*

Above *Although each of these napkins is a different colour they are recognizably a matching set, unified by their woven design of fine white stripes.*

Left *Bands of broad and narrow blue stripes on white linen napkins and dish towels are a classic style, equally at home in a country kitchen or a city flat. Matching striped linens with blue-striped white china gives a co-ordinated look.*

Above *A deep blue and white napkin in a contemporary style creates a very cool mood when combined with stark white plates and plain glasses on a bright white tablecloth.*

Above *Blue and white checks and stripes can be mixed endlessly and never fight with one another, so you can expand your collection over time with bric-à-brac finds.*

Antique

Old fabrics have a quality that is hard to match today, and antique linen that has been laundered many times has a softness and colour that is impossible to replicate. Many antique napkins are also beautifully decorated with drawn threadwork or embroidery, with handstitching of outstanding quality. If you enjoy hunting in antique shops and on bric-à-brac stalls, small-scale textiles of this kind are easily affordable and rewarding to collect. There's no need to buy a complete matching set. Old linens look wonderful when mixed together, so you can add to your collection whenever you see pieces you like, building up a unique harlequin set of beautiful napkins.

Above *This antique French dish towel has been folded to make a charming napkin "book" held in place by the string fastener, in which napkins can be kept until needed on the table.*

Above *An embroidered napkin is quickly turned into a charming pocket by turning in the corners and catching the edges in place. A flower-shaped button provides the finishing touch.*

Right *Mix and match antique napkins with an assortment of decorative finishes – their colour and the quality of the linen will ensure that they all look lovely together.*

Below *Whitework embroidery adds a luxurious touch to any place setting.*

Traditional

Classic and delicate china tableware, of the kind that we usually associate with a more traditional era and styling, has a charm of its own. With designs and colour schemes of every imaginable kind, napkins need to be carefully matched to ensure that colours and designs will not clash visually once on the table. For many designs, particularly old chinaware, plain white napkins may be the best choice. These may be embellished with embroidery, decorative scalloped edges or patterns in drawn threadwork. Very decorative napkins should be folded simply. If they have an embroidered monongram in one corner, fold them so that this is displayed. If you are trying to match new napkins to old china that has a busy pattern, try to match the colourway first, keeping the linen plain for visual simplicity and an elegant table setting.

Above Geometric patterns such as checks blend happily with a mixture of different floral prints if you choose designs that are of a similar scale and colour.

Below Plain white cotton or linen napkins are classic and timeless, decorated with traditional drawn threadwork. They are the perfect choice if you have tableware in elaborate floral designs.

Above Old-fashioned floral printed napkins have the right traditional feel for a well-appointed summer picnic: use them to line baskets for transporting china and food to your picnic spot.

Oriental tables

The simplicity and harmony of Oriental table settings provide a welcome antidote to today's increasingly demanding lifestyles: plain plates and folded napkins in neutral or earth colours are positioned with geometric rigour and little adornment on bare tables. If this is too stark for your taste, you could choose a white or neutral cloth and add a single flower or stem in a glass or porcelain vase, trimmed with a twist of raffia.

This elegant, restrained look can turn a quick stir-fry into a special occasion, although you do not have to wait until you are accomplished with a wok before you give it a try.

Strict attention to detail is the key to this look: everything on the table should be perfectly placed and aligned. Napkins need to be carefully pressed and beautifully folded or rolled, creating a sense of order and calm.

Above Inspired by origami, this Japanese-style napkin fold has a sculptural look and its rolled central section makes a perfect holder for a place card and a tiny sprig of flowers.

Above A matt black bowl provides elegant contrast with a coarsely woven napkin in natural cream, precisely rolled. The beargrass-wrapped stone provides a touch of Japanese styling.

Right Classic white napkins are easily incorporated with a spare Oriental style if they are faultlessly pressed, simply folded or rolled and precisely placed on the table.

Above *Chopsticks tied with raffia and placed with precision on toning napkins give a buffet party table an Eastern look, but you could achieve a similar effect with sets of knives and forks.*

Above *For a more relaxed, country style, still with an Oriental influence, combine bamboo-handled cutlery, woven rush plates and terracotta glazed bowls with neutral-coloured napkins.*

Above *The delicacy and fine lines of matt-textured Oriental porcelain is enhanced when accessorized with luxuriously thick table napkins in strong, earthy colours.*

Making and decorating napkins

Exquisite edging, delicate embroidery, or a simple motif painted on to one corner can transform a simple square of fabric into a delightful napkin that is all the more gorgeous for the handcrafted detail. The joy is that napkins are small enough for an embroidery detail to be completed with gratifying speed.

Inspirational ideas

Easy edgings and simple decorative effects can transform plain napkins into something unique and special. Most involve only plain machine stitching or simple hand sewing, and none takes very long. You could also look for interesting ready-made trimmings and decorative materials such as ribbons and beads, or even little jewels to add a sparkle to your festive table.

Above *A little glass bead adds a different colour to a traditional cutwork daisy.*

Above *A border of self-coloured straight stitches finishes this napkin elegantly.*

Above *Linen and natural raffia make a great modern partnership.*

Above *Fine lilac organdie takes on a very feminine feel with this picot edging.*

Above *A narrow crochet trim is charming while avoiding any hint of frilliness.*

Above *Pretty shell discs on a ready-made trim are easy to sew on a toning napkin.*

Above *White lingerie trimmings have an alternative use adorning plain napkins.*

Above *Pearl buttons threaded on to plain household string make a stunning edging.*

Above *Four lines of straight stitching in blue look smart on plain white napkins.*

Above *A border of toile de jouy applied to linen napkins of a similar, but plain fabric gives a subtle but colourful effect.*

Above *Decorative satin ribbons can be used in all kinds of ways to add charming decoration to napkins.*

Above *The narrowest braid border adds richness to a linen napkin.*

Above *Nothing could be simpler than finishing plain napkins with frayed edges.*

Above *The beads on this coffee-coloured napkin set off the modern cutlery well.*

Making a plain napkin

If you need napkins in a specific colour or fabric, it can be easier and cheaper to buy a length of fabric and make your own. Choose linen or cotton in a firm, plain weave that will not pull out of shape, and follow the weave carefully when cutting out your squares.

MATERIALS

For each napkin:

- **Plain fabric 50cm/20in square**
- **Scissors**
- **Needle and tacking (basting) thread**
- **Sewing machine or needle and matching thread**

1 To cut out the napkin, snip into the selvage and pull a thread, then cut along the line. Measure 50cm/20in along the edge and repeat to cut the remaining sides of the square. Press under a narrow turning on each side, then press under a hem allowance of, say, 1cm/½in.

2 Unfold the pressed creases and turn the fabric in at 45 degrees at each corner so that the folds line up. Press each corner firmly to mark the diagonal line. Unfold the corners and trim them at 45 degrees, a short distance outside the diagonal crease.

3 Refold and press each of the creases then tack (baste) the hem and mitred corners in place. Stitch the hem by hand or machine. Slip stitch the mitres together, working from the corners inwards. Remove the tacking stitches and press.

Making a bound-edge napkin

A contrast binding is a classic way to finish the edge of a napkin. Use a fairly thin fabric to make the binding so that the finished corners are not too bulky and the binding can be easily stitched in place with a sewing machine. This is a very simple project to make.

1 To cut the main fabric, snip into the selvage and pull a thread, then cut along the line. Measure 38cm/15in along the selvage and repeat the process. Measure along the cut edge and pull a thread to complete the square.

2 Press the strips for the binding in half lengthwise, with wrong sides together, then fold the long raw edges of each strip in to the centre and press again.

3 Place strips of binding down two opposite sides of the napkin and tack (baste) in place, checking that you catch the binding in the stitching on both sides. Stitch close to the folded edge.

4 Trim the ends of the binding flush with the edges of the napkin. Pin the other two pieces of binding in place. Turn the short ends in at the corners and tack. Stitch as before, reverse-stitching at each end.

MATERIALS

For each napkin:

- **38cm/15in square of fabric**
- **Scissors**
- **Measuring tape**
- **4 x 40cm/1½ x 16in of fabric for the binding**
- **Pins**
- **Needle and tacking (basting) thread**
- **Sewing machine and matching thread**

Cutlery roll

Smart braid and clever folding transform a plain napkin into a neat roll to hold a set of cutlery – perfect for picnicking. Cleverly accommodating a four-piece place setting plus acting as a napkin, the rolls can be filled up for each guest before setting out for your picnic, or stacked neatly on a buffet table.

MATERIALS

For each cutlery roll:

- **1 large napkin, 50cm/20in square**
- **52cm/21in braid 4cm/1½in wide for binding**
- **Scissors**
- **Pins, needle and tacking (basting) thread**
- **Sewing machine and matching thread**
- **2.7m/3yd matching braid 2cm/¾in wide for top edge, sides and ties**

1 Cut a piece of the wider braid the same length as one side of the napkin. Place it along the edge of the napkin. Pin and tack (baste) in position, then machine stitch along both edges of the braid.

2 Place the napkin face down and fold up the braid-finished edge of the napkin to a depth that will hold the knife, fork and spoon. Cut two lengths of narrow braid to fit along the top edge of the roll. Pin one to the front of the top edge and the other to the back. Stitch through all three layers along both edges of the braid. Repeat with both side seams, tacking through all the layers to join the sides. Place the cutlery over the top of the folded edge and use pins to mark the positions of the stitching lines.

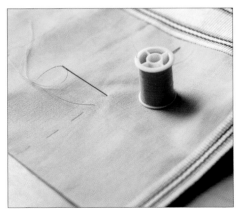

3 When you are happy with the spacing of the cutlery, tack the seams between the pockets and remove the pins. Machine stitch the seams, firmly securing each one at the top of the wide braid using a reverse stitch. Remove the tacking threads.

4 To make the ties, fold the remaining piece of narrow braid in half and pin in position halfway down one side between the two napkin layers. Stitch through all the layers along the narrow braid to join the seams. Turn in narrow double hems at the ends of the ties, and stitch.

Napkin pocket

Transform simple napkins into exquisite pockets for storing linens in scented cupboards or drawers. A plain piqué cotton napkin can be made to look very special with clever folding and the addition of an imaginative fastener. With the hems already finished off, there is little fiddly sewing to be done.

MATERIALS

- **White piqué napkin, approximately 45cm/18in square**
- **Needle and matching thread**
- **Ready-made rolled fastener**

1 Fold the napkin in half and then in half again, and run your thumb down the folds to make strong creases. Unfold, then fold the corners to the centre so they meet where the original creases cross. Make sure all the edges meet together accurately, then press.

2 Slip stitch the edges together down two sides of one point, leaving the opposite side open like the flap of an envelope. Make extra stitches where the corners meet, for extra strength.

3 Sew one part of the rolled fastener on to the loose flap and mark where it will join the other part of the fastener on the sewn section. Stitch the fastener firmly into position.

Drawn threadwork

For classic elegance, there is no better decoration for napkins than drawn threadwork. It is often used to stunning effect on banqueting linens. Choose an even-weave fabric that is made from strong fibres, otherwise they will keep snapping as you try to pull them out. Linen is ideal.

MATERIALS

For each napkin:

- **Linen 60cm/24in square**
- **Pins**
- **Needle and contrasting and matching threads**

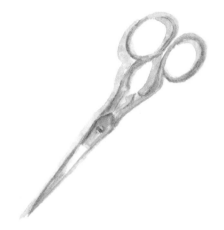

1 Using pins, mark out lines 6cm/2½in in from each edge. Since the hem will be turned back to the drawn threadwork, this will give a finished border of 3cm/1¼in. Turn the hem back to the line of pins to check the result. Make a line of tacking (basting) stitches in contrasting thread in place of the pins.

2 Working inside the pinned area, carefully ease out one strand of the weave right the way across the fabric. Repeat this process, ensuring that the number of threads that are withdrawn is divisible by three. Repeat on all sides, pulling out an equal number of threads each time.

3 Turn in and press a narrow hem all around the raw edges, then fold this hemmed edge back to the line of withdrawn threads to make a double border. Press and tack in place. Mitre the corners (see Making a plain napkin). With the wrong side of the napkin towards you, work hem stitches, catching three threads at a time and taking in the edge of the hem as you go. Repeat all along the top edge of the drawn threads and then all along the lower edge, lining up the stitches to create a neat row of holes.

Appliqué napkin

Decorating with appliqué does not have to be intricate, complex or time-consuming. Even the simplest design, used to trim the edge of a napkin, can give it a more finished look. Use ready-made napkins or make them yourself from squares of fabric, and use the same fabric in a different colour for the appliqué.

MATERIALS

For each napkin:

- **Lime green napkin**
- **Scissors**
- **Tape measure**
- **Paper**
- **Needle and matching thread**
- **Yellow napkin**

1 Cut a 5cm/2in strip from the lime napkin. Fold the strip in half three times. Cut a piece of paper to the size of this quarter-fold, and then fold the paper in half and snip off one corner. Open out the paper and use it as a template to cut the corners of the folded lime strip. Open out the zigzag edging.

2 Turn in a 6mm/¼in hem along the long straight side of the lime strip and along the short ends. Press. Slip stitch the straight edge and the ends of the lime strip to the edges of the yellow napkin.

3 Slip stitch the zigzag edge of the strip to the napkin, turning in the edges as you go. You will need to turn in these edges only very slightly – just enough to neaten them – or you may find it difficult to create the points at the inner and outer corners of the zigzag.

Couched organza

Gossamer light and delicately translucent, organza has surprising body. It is naturally stiff, which means you can not only create light, luminous folds, but you can also crease it to a knife-edged sharpness. Couch a simple motif into one corner of each napkin for a pretty, embossed effect.

MATERIALS

- **Ready-made napkin in silk organza**
- **Tracing paper**
- **Fine felt-tipped pen**
- **Masking tape**
- **Dressmaking pencil**
- **Fine cotton string**
- **Needle and matching thread**
- **Scissors**

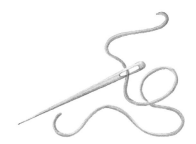

1 Press the napkin flat. Trace the motif from the back of the book using tracing paper and a felt-tipped pen. When the ink has completely dried, tape the motif on to a flat surface and place the hemmed napkin over the top, positioning the corner over the motif. Tape the napkin in position to fix both the tracing paper and the fabric firmly. Using a dressmaking pencil, trace the motif on to the corner of the napkin. Remove the masking tape securing the napkin.

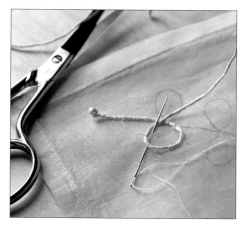

2 ◁ Knot the end of a piece of cotton string and lay the string along the traced design on the corner of the napkin. Using the needle and thread, neatly couch the string in position. When you near the end of the motif, make a knot at this end of the string, trim and stitch down neatly. Iron the couched motif string-side down on a towel, to avoid flattening the string.

Pearl-trimmed appliquéd cupids

If you want to create an outrageously romantic table dressing for a meal on a special Valentine's day or for a personal celebration, these engaging little cupids will provide a perfect finishing touch. Stitch them to the corners of silk organza napkins, then decorate their wings with tiny pearls.

MATERIALS

For each napkin:

- **50cm/18in square of white silk organza**
- **Pins**
- **Needle and white thread**
- **Tracing paper**
- **Pencil**
- **Paper**
- **Scissors**
- **Scrap of muslin or tulle**
- **6 seed-pearl beads**

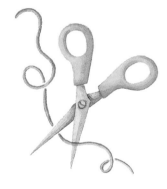

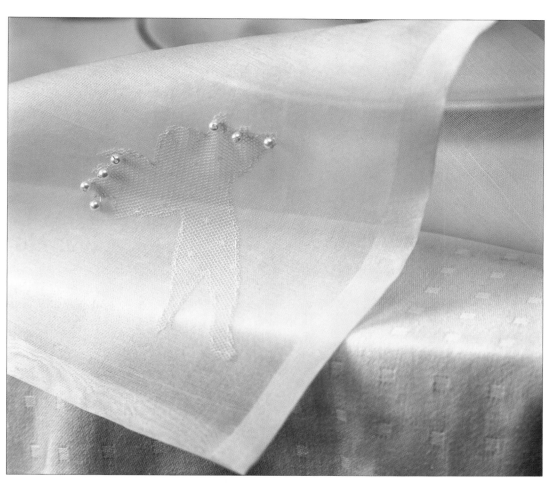

1 Turn in a narrow double hem all round the edge of the organza, press and slip stitch in place, mitring the corners. Trace the cupid at the back of the book and cut out a template. Pin the template to the muslin or tulle and cut out.

2 Sew the cupid to one corner of the napkin using tiny running stitches. Do this as neatly as you can, so that the stitches are invisible.

3 Sew three seed-pearl beads to each wing tip of the cupid.

Cross-stitch napkin

For good-looking cross stitch the stitches must be completely regular, so checked or gingham fabric makes an ideal ready-made grid. This very easy project is ideal if you have not done much embroidery before. The bold stitches would also add a hand-made quality to a set of bought table napkins.

MATERIALS

For each napkin:

- **Heavyweight checked cotton fabric, 48cm/19in square**
- **Pins**
- **Needle and tacking (basting) thread**
- **Sewing machine and matching thread**
- **Stranded embroidery cotton (floss) in a bright contrast colour**

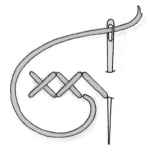

Above *Cross stitch*

1 Turn under the raw edge on each edge of the fabric square, then fold over again to make a narrow hem. Pin and tack (baste), turning in the corners neatly.

2 Machine stitch the double hem in place with a matching thread using straight or zigzag stitch.

3 Thread the needle with all six strands of a length of embroidery cotton (floss) double the width of the napkin and knot the end. Leaving a blank row of checks, start at one end of a row with the knot on the wrong side. Stitch diagonally across alternate squares to the end of the row. Finish with a double stitch.

4 Rethread the needle as before, then work back along the same row, crossing over each diagonal stitch. Repeat to make a pattern of three cross-stitch rows at opposite ends of the napkin.

Lemon slice napkin

This lovely bright yellow napkin, embroidered with a succulent lemon slice, would look delightful on a table set for a summer lunch in the garden. If you're embroidering a whole set of napkins you could vary the colours of the stitches to make slices of lime and orange.

MATERIALS

For each napkin:

- **Tracing paper**
- **Soft and hard pencils**
- **Scissors**
- **Pins**
- **Large yellow napkin**
- **Needle and stranded embroidery cotton (floss) in dark and pale yellow, off-white and dark green**

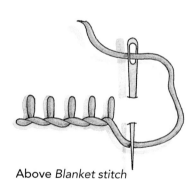

Above *Blanket stitch*

1 Trace the template at the back of the book and draw over the lemon motif on the reverse of the tracing with a soft pencil. Pin the tracing in the corner of the napkin and transfer the motif.

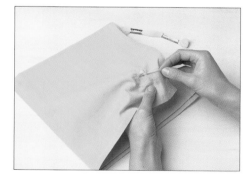

2 Using dark yellow thread, make French knots in the centre of the lemon. Fill the segments in pale yellow stem stitch. Fill the pith in off-white stem stitch, and the skin area with dark yellow French knots. Work dark yellow stem stitch around the edge of the pith and another row outside that in green. Work a dark green running stitch around the French knots and add some small dark green stitches as shading in the segments.

3 Work dark green blanket stitch around the hem of the napkin. The stitches can be worked over the existing machine stitching. Press the embroidery on the reverse side.

Shell-edge napkin

Undyed linen is perfect for table settings with a seashore theme. Buy ready-made napkins or make your own, then trim them with a small shell at each corner, or stitch shells all the way along two opposite sides. The shells will need to have small holes drilled through the tops.

MATERIALS

For each napkin:

- **Undyed linen, about 48cm/19in square**
- **Tape measure**
- **Pins**
- **Sewing machine and matching thread**
- **Needle**
- **Cream cotton perle embroidery thread**
- **16 shells**
- **Length of fine wire**

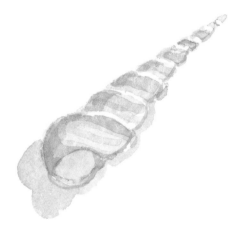

1 Turn in a double hem on all sides of the fabric and press. Mitre the corners and stitch in place. Thread the cotton perle through the shells by first making a large knot at one end of a length of doubled thread. Bend the wire in half and thread the looped end down through the shell. Pass the knotted thread through this.

2 Draw the wire back through the shell, pulling the thread with it. The knotted end should stay securely inside the shell. This process can be a little fiddly, and it works better with some shells than others.

3 Thread the embroidery needle with the unknotted end of the doubled embroidery thread and pass the needle through from the back of the napkin, round the back of the thread at the top of the shell, and through to the back of the napkin to fasten off.

Monograms

Adding a monogram to a napkin is a luxurious touch of ownership. Make them as a wedding gift incorporating the initial of couple's first names. Keep the lettering simple and modern or for antique fabrics find an ornate typescript with swirly letters.

MATERIALS

For each napkin:

- **48cm/19in even-weave linen**
- **Stranded embroidery cotton (floss) in one or two colours**
- **Seed beads**
- **Light box**
- **Fabric marker**

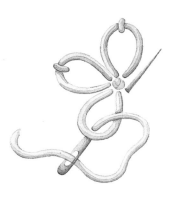

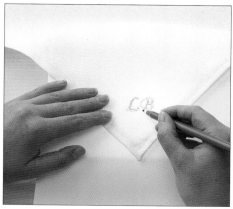

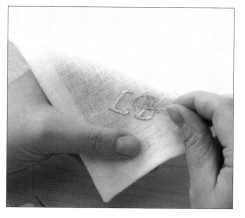

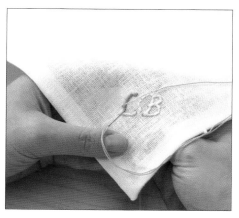

1 Make up the napkin following the instructions for Making a Plain Napkin. Arrange the letters of your choice under one corner of the napkin and place both on top of light source. Transfer the letters using the fabric marker pen.

2 To pad the stitching, make short diagonal satin stitches inside the marked lines of the lettering.

3 Oversew the padding stitches with satin stitch in your choice of colour, this time covering the lines of the letters. Lazy daisy flowers and a scattering of seed beads add pretty decorative details.

Cross-stitch heart

Bold and simple, cross stitch has the naive charm of folk art and is easy to do provided you keep the stitches regular. Here it is used to embroider a heart on a plain napkin.

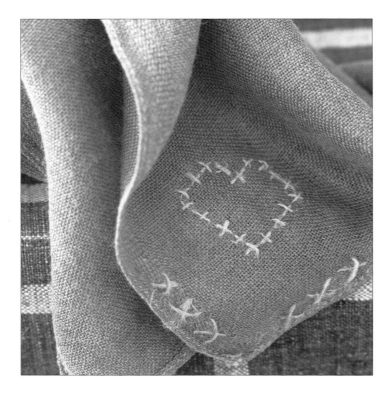

MATERIALS

For each napkin:

• **Pencil, tissue paper and pins**

• **Plain napkin**

• **Needle and stranded embroidery cotton (floss)**

1 Draw a heart in even-sized crosses on a small piece of tissue paper. Pin the paper to the corner of the napkin, then stitch over the crosses.

2 Carefully tear away the tissue paper, leaving the stitched design on the napkin. If any small pieces of paper remain caught under the stitches, use the point of the needle to remove them.

Beaded napkin

This vivid orange linen napkin has been embellished with a row of tiny running stitches in co-ordinating tapestry wool, finished off with a few fine orange beads at each corner.

MATERIALS

For each napkin:

• **Napkin**

• **Orange tapestry wool**

• **Tapestry needle**

• **Scissors**

• **20 small orange beads**

1 Make small running stiches in wool around the napkin border, threading on beads where desired. Here, five evenly spaced beads finish off each corner.

Simple stitching

Used cleverly, embroidery stitches can look highly effective on a plain napkin. Running stitch, French knots and daisy stitch have all been employed here to create a French provincial style.

1 Turn under 1cm/½in around all edges of the chambray and press. Turn under a 4cm/1½in hem and mitre the corners. Slip stitch the hems in place. Press. Using six strands of blue embroidery thread (floss), make large running stitches 2.5cm/1in from the edge all around the napkin. Make another row 5mm/¼in away from the outside edge.

2 Mark the position of the the daisies and French knots. The French knots are positioned in each corner, and then every 10cm/4in, centred between the lines. Using six strands of red thread, make the French knots. Using six strands of blue thread, work daisy stitches between the French knots. Press the napkin on the wrong side.

MATERIALS

For each napkin:

• **Cotton chambray, 60cm/24in square**

• **Tape measure**

• **Needle and matching thread**

• **Blue and red stranded embroidery cotton (floss)**

Ric-rac braid

Grosgrain ribbon teamed with contrasting ric-rac trim gives a smart yet pretty edging to plain napkin. You will need a sewing machine or very neat hand stitching for this project.

MATERIALS

For each napkin:

• **2m/2¼yd grosgrain ribbon 2.5cm/1in wide**

• **Scissors**

• **Pins**

• **Plain napkin, 50cm/20in square**

• **Needle and tacking (basting) thread**

• **Sewing machine**

• **2m/2¼yd ric-rac trim**

1 Cut four 50cm/20in lengths of grosgrain ribbon. Pin along opposite edges of the napkin, turning under the ends. Pin, tack (baste), then stitch all around. Repeat with the remaining two sides.

2 Pin and tack the ric-rac so it overlaps the edge of the ribbon where it meets the napkin. At the corners, manipulate the ric-rac so that it forms a continuous piece. Sew in place, turning the ends in.

Easy embroidery

Simple embroidery can make a very effective edging for a set of napkins, especially if you choose strong colours and make the stitches large for a bold, modern statement. Blanket stitch, oversized oversewing and cross stitch are all easy to do; the knack is to keep the stitches evenly spaced.

MATERIALS

For each napkin:

- **Plain even-weave napkin**
- **Needle**
- **Stranded embroidery cotton (floss) in a toning or contrasting colour**
- **Scissors**

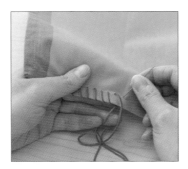

1 Oversewing is easy to do. Simply thread a length of cotton on to a needle and knot one end. With the knot on the wrong side of the napkin make large stitches from the back to the front.

2 Blanket stitch is a well-known favourite stitch that provides a neat edging. Keep the stitches large and use a thick thread so that the work is quickly completed.

3 Cross-stitch is one of the quickest stitches to make and can be used to add a hint of contrasting colour to a bright napkin for a truly contemporary feel.

CROSS-STITCH

Cross-stitch worked in magenta on a bright orange napkin creates a strong contemporary colour scheme. Choose a ready-made napkin with an even weave and a rough, homespun texture, and use the machine-stitched hem around the edge to guide your embroidery stitches. Work with six strands of embroidery cotton (floss) and make the crosses up to 1cm/½in wide for a bold effect.

Hand-painted motif

If you don't enjoy sewing you can use paint to decorate plain napkins. There is a large choice of suitable fabric paints and pens, specially designed so that the finished work can be pressed with a hot iron to set the colour. Use paints for bold all-over designs, thick pens for strong lines and fine pens for details.

MATERIALS

For each napkin:

- **Tracing paper**
- **Black felt-tipped pen**
- **Dressmaker's carbon**
- **Plain white napkin**
- **Fabric pens in black and yellow**

1 Trace the bee template at the back of the book using a black felt-tipped pen. Place dressmaker's carbon over the corner of the napkin with the traced design over the top. Draw over the design to transfer it to the fabric.

2 Draw in the traced outline with a black fabric-dye pen, then fill in with a yellow fabric-dye pen. When dry, iron to fix the dye.

Clover leaf tablecloth and napkin

This fresh four-leaf clover pattern is made with a potato print. The cut potato exudes a starchy liquid that blends into the ink and adds translucence. The best fabric to print on is 100 per cent cotton or natural fabric, pre-washed to remove any glaze or stiffener.

MATERIALS

- **Medium-size fresh potato**
- **Sharp knife and cutting board**
- **Small artist's paintbrush**
- **Craft knife**
- **Leaf green water-based block printing fabric ink**
- **Sheet of glass**
- **Palette knife**
- **Small gloss paint roller**
- **White 100 per cent cotton tablecloth and napkins, washed and ironed**
- **Matching thread**
- **Sewing machine**

1 Cut the potato in half in one stroke to give a flat surface. Paint the clover leaf shape on the cut surface of the potato. Cut around the shape using a craft knife.

2 Cut around the internal shapes. Scoop out the potato flesh with the end of the knife blade. Cut away the waste potato to a depth of 6mm/¼in.

3 Squeeze some printing ink on to the sheet of glass and run the roller over it until it is thoroughly coated. Apply an even coating of ink to the potato stamp.

4 Arrange the tablecloth and napkins on a waterproof surface and print the pattern at random. Re-ink the potato after every two printings to vary the intensity of the colour. Leave the finished fabric to dry then press to set the design.

Painted "cross-stitch" napkin

This clever imitation of cross-stitch can be achieved quickly and easily with one colour of fabric paint and a fine artist's paintbrush. Instead of sewing the running stitches around the hem you could paint these too if you prefer. To make the project even simpler you could use ready-made napkins.

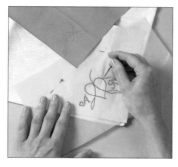

1 Turn in the raw edges of the linen square and press a 1cm/½in hem. Mitre the corners and press. Tack (baste) the hem and stitch in place.
  Trace the heart template provided and the required letters for the monogram.

2 Place the tracing on the corner of the napkin 2.5cm/1in from the edges. Put a piece of dressmaker's carbon paper under the tracing, chalk-side down. Pin. With an embroidery needle, prick through both layers of paper, making closely spaced holes along the lines of the pattern to transfer the image.

3 Mix a heaped tablespoonful of cerise fabric paint with a teaspoonful of fabric medium. Using a fine paintbrush and following the lines of the transfer, paint a series of small crosses to give the illusion of cross stitch. Leave to dry.

4 With a length of stranded embroidery cotton split into three strands, sew a running stitch over the machine stitching around the hem. Using a warm dry iron, press the back of each napkin to set the paint and iron the napkin flat.

MATERIALS

For each napkin:

- **White linen, 52cm/21in square**
- **Scissors**
- **Pins**
- **Needle and tacking (basting) thread**
- **Sewing machine and matching thread**
- **Tracing paper and pencil**
- **Dressmaker's carbon**
- **Large embroidery needle**
- **Cerise fabric paint**
- **Fabric medium**
- **Fine artist's paintbrush**
- **Stranded embroidery cotton (floss) to match paint**

Napkin rings

With imagination and creativity, napkins can be dressed with rings and all kinds of ties fashioned from a wide variety of materials, selected to complement the table setting and inspire your guests. Attention to detail will help to create a special dining environment.

Inspirational ideas

Dress up your napkins with original rings and ties to create table settings with a sense of occasion. The same linens can take on quite different personalities depending on whether they are clasped with a sparkling jewel, trimmed with beads or tied with ribbons and a seasonal flower. Napkin rings can be bought in many styles, or made from wire or natural materials.

Above *A diamanté buckle makes a glamorous ring for a pale pink napkin.*

Above *A curled pipe cleaner is a novel and very simply made napkin ring.*

Above *White tape trimmed with shells is an inexpensive and easy napkin tie.*

Above *Twisted twigs threaded with beads look stunning around white linen.*

Above *A flamboyant cerise bow contrasts beautifully with a purple napkin.*

Above *An assortment of glass beads on fine wire have a jewel-like appearance.*

Above *Single hydrangea florets look delicately pretty on pale green napkins.*

Above *Narrow satin ribbon is simply knotted with a tiny flower sprig tucked in.*

Above *A row of silk daisies looks enchanting around a striped napkin.*

Above *Ordinary piping cord, finger-knitted into a simple chain, perfectly complements blue and white checked cotton.*

Above *This lovely flower is made from brightly coloured beads threaded on wire and is attached to a spiral ring of silver wire.*

Above *Buttoned-up string in pistachio green looks fresh and contemporary.*

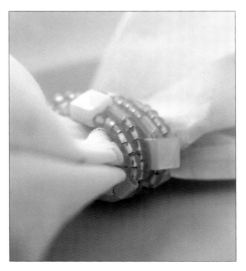

Above *Strings of pearly beads look stylish tied around a classic white napkin.*

Above *Lustrous plaited cord gives a Celtic touch to elegant grey linen napkins.*

Orchid napkin tie

The elegant shape of a perfect white orchid head makes a delicate but sophisticated napkin tie – the perfect complement to pure white linen. This exotic flower would look lovely as part of an all-white table setting, with the dark green leaves adding just the right amount of definition to the design.

MATERIALS

For each napkin:

- **25cm/10in narrow off-white ribbon**
- **2 leaves**
- **1 orchid or other similar white flower**

1 Loosely pleat the napkin to fit on the plate. Make a tuck in it if the napkin is too large.

2 Loosely tie the narrow ribbon around the middle of the napkin.

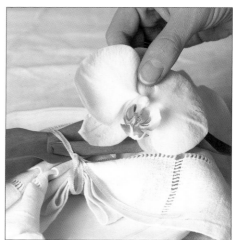

3 Carefully tuck the leaves into the ribbon, then add the flower.

Riveted leaf napkin ring

Any large, leathery leaves can be quickly transformed into napkin rings. These are made from the enormous leaves of *Fatsia japonica*, an evergreen that puts on astounding growth in spring. Riveting them together is both quick and easy, using a small riveting kit available at a haberdashery.

MATERIALS

For each napkin:

- *Fatsia japonica* **leaf, or similar**
- **Secateurs (pruners)**
- **2 rivets**
- **Riveting pliers**

1 Fold the napkin into a triangle and roll the ends into the middle.

2 Choose a half-grown leaf, as it will retain its bright green shade and be at its most pliable. Cut off the stalk of the leaf you have selected.

3 Wrap the leaf around the napkin. Secure in position by riveting the sides together using riveting pliers.

Scented napkin ring

Inspired by hair "scrunchies", these cardamom-filled organza napkin rings make elegant yet inexpensive table accessories. Cardamom is a perfect spice to use for the filling. With its fresh, sweet perfume it will enhance the ambience of the table without overwhelming the aroma of the food.

MATERIALS

For each napkin ring:

- **Metal-shot organza, 46 x 15cm/18 x 6in**
- **15cm/6in elastic**
- **Needle and matching thread**
- **Bodkin or safety pin**
- **Green cardamom pods**

1 Fold the organza strip in half lengthwise, with right sides together. Stitch a 5mm/¼in seam down the long edge to form a tube. Turn right-side out.

2 Turn in the raw edge at one short end of the organza and tack (baste). Use the bodkin or safety pin to thread the elastic through the organza tube and stitch the two ends of elastic together.

3 Loosely fill the scrunchie with a handful of green cardamom pods.

4 Tuck the raw edge of the organza tube under the basted edge, and slip stitch the two ends of the tube together to enclose the filling. Make sure you match the seams at the join.

Buttoned wrap

Edge and encircle napkins with a beautiful fabric loop and create real chic by securing it with a natural mother-of-pearl button. You need only a small amount of fabric so buy the very best for exquisite results. Make different colours and individualize a wrap for each member of the family.

MATERIALS

For each napkin ring:

- **Strip of fabric, 10 x 17cm/4 x 6¾in**
- **Pins**
- **Needle and thread**
- **Tape measure**
- **Scissors**
- **Sewing machine**
- **Mother-of-pearl button, 2cm/¾in in diameter**

1 Fold the fabric in half with right sides together to form a strip measuring 5 x 17cm/2 x 6¾in. Pin, tack (baste) and stitch a 5mm/¼in seam down the long edge. Fold the strip in half lengthwise to find the centre of a short edge, and place a pin at this point. At one end, measure 3cm/1¼in from the top down each side of the strip, and place a pin on each side of the strip. Use these pins as markers from which to cut the end to a point, then square off the tip. Stitch a 5mm/¼in seam around the pointed end.

2 Turn right-side out. Turn under 5mm/¼in at the straight end of the strip and slip stitch together. Press. Work a line of machine stitching close to the edge around the whole wrap for a neat finish. Make a machine-stitched buttonhole at the pointed end to fit the mother-of-pearl button and stitch the button in position at the straight end.

Celebrate with paper

Cost effective, cheerful and with an infinite variety of colours and finishes, paper napkin rings can add fun to any party. Browse around art stores for special hand-made paper, but you can achieve original effects with the most everyday materials, such as brown wrapping paper and corrugated cardboard.

MATERIALS

For each napkin ring:

- **Thick paper in dark blue and lime green**
- **Ruler**
- **PVA (white) glue**
- **Craft knife and cutting mat**

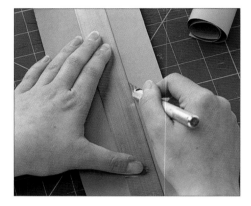

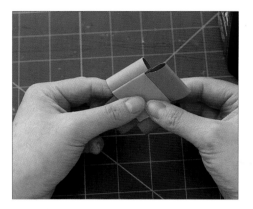

1 Using the ruler as a straightedge, cut two strips of blue paper about 15cm/6in long and 2.5cm/1in wide. Using one strip to form the napkin ring, lap one end over the other and glue.

2 Bring the ends of the second strip to the middle and glue. Tear a short strip of lime green paper and glue it around the centre of the bow. Glue the whole bow to the napkin ring.

OTHER CREATIVE WAYS WITH PAPER

Concertina ring

Crease a sheet of paper concertina-style into 2.5cm/1in widths along its length, then tear it into strips to give slightly rough edges. Punch holes through all the layers. Test the ring for length around a napkin, then thread coloured paper ribbon through the holes and tie.

Layered paper ring

Tear a 15cm/6in strip of paper, 2.5cm/1in wide. Tear a slightly shorter and narrower length of contrasting paper and glue this centrally on top of the first strip. Add a torn paper square in the centre. Once the napkin ring is dry, punch a hole in each end, thread string through and tie to secure.

Paper fan

Fans lend a touch of frivolity to a party table. Simply concertina a small piece of paper, fold in half and glue the centre together to form the fan, then glue the whole ensemble on to a basic paper napkin ring.

Paper star

Crisp and smart, there is something rather lovely about the juxtaposition of pure white paper with traditional starched linen. Paper napkin rings may be throwaway, but with a little imagination and good sharp creases, they can be made to look very special indeed.

MATERIALS

For each napkin ring:

- **Sheet of A4 cartridge paper (29 x 42cm/11½ x 16½in)**
- **Scissors**
- **Strong white thread or fine wire**
- **Double-sided tape**
- **Paper glue (optional)**

Paper lantern

Cut a piece of paper 21 x 15cm/8½ x 6in. Fold it in half lengthwise and make a series of cuts 1cm/½in apart from the folded side of the paper, finishing the cuts about 2.5cm/1in before you reach the edges of the paper. Unfold the paper and bend into a ring. Stick the short edges together to complete the lantern.

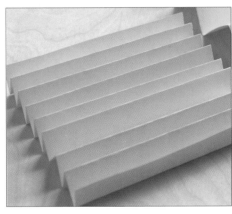

1 Cut a sheet of cartridge paper in half crosswise and fold one half into narrow accordion pleats. Press firmly on each fold to ensure sharp creases. From the remaining paper cut a 2.5cm/1in-wide strip to form the napkin ring.

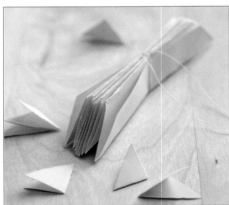

2 Secure the pleated paper tightly in the centre with a piece of thread or fine wire. Snip diagonally across both ends of the pleats to form points.

3 Fan out the pleated paper to form a complete star. Pinch the two end points together at each side and fold over once to secure the star shape. Join the ends of the paper strip with double-sided tape to form a napkin ring, then tape or glue this to the back of the star.

Foil place tag

Avoid awkward moments when seating guests by giving every setting a place name. Luggage style labels, crafted from foil, are practical, pleasing and give a modern twist to classic white table linen. The silver of the tags complements the tableware perfectly.

MATERIALS

For each tag:

- **2 pieces of modelling foil, each 4 x 6cm/1½ x 2¼ in**
- **Double-sided tape**
- **Embossing tool or empty ballpoint pen**
- **Hole punch**
- **Silver ribbon**
- **Cutting mat**

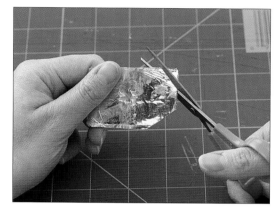

1 Stick the two pieces of modelling foil together using double-sided tape to make the label more substantial. Trim off the two top corners at 45 degrees to create a traditional luggage-label shape.

2 Emboss the design with your guest's initials or name using an embossing tool or empty ballpoint pen. Punch a hole in the top of the tag and thread the silver ribbon through, then tie around the napkin.

Fine wirework

It is always thrilling when you find a way to transform the most ordinary household items into something quite beautiful. If it is quick and easy, so much the better. These simple ideas using twisted fine wire fall right into that category, and make wonderful napkin holders.

MATERIALS

For each napkin ring:

- **Length of two-core black electrical wire**
- **Wire cutters**
- **Small pliers (optional)**
- **Fine wire**

1 Separate the two-core wire by tearing the strips apart. Cut a length of wire about 15cm/6in long for the body of the dragonfly, fold it in half and twist the two ends together.

2 Make two large loops by wrapping the wire round your hand and twist at the base to form wings. Twist the ends of the wire around the body near the looped end.

3 Bend a length of fine wire into a circle to create a napkin ring. Twist the ends together to join and wrap them around the dragonfly's body. Trim the ends.

OTHER CREATIVE WAYS WITH WIRE

Hovering bee

Turn in one end of a piece of galvanized wire, then wrap the wire a few times around a cylindrical object, such as a rolling pin, depending on how tight you want the spiral to be. Remove the mould, cut the wire leaving an elongated end, and attach an ornament to the end of the wire.

Plaited ring

Divide a length of two-core electrical wire into single strips by tearing it down the middle. Cut a strand into three equal lengths and plait loosely to make a band of the required length. Trim the ends and twist them together to make a ring. Finish by glueing on a silver bead.

A trio of medallions

Divide a length of two-core electrical wire as before and twist it tightly into three small coils. Use a second length of wire to wrap around the coils to secure them, looping them together as you do so. Loop the top coil to a ring of fine wire to hold the napkin.

Fretwork-style felt

Felt doesn't fray, so it can be cut into intricate shapes – and there is no need to hem around fiddly corners. Equipped with the sharpest scissors you can find, there is no end to the designs you can cut.

MATERIALS

For each napkin ring:

- **Felt squares in two contrasting colours**
- **Tape measure**
- **Sharp embroidery scissors**
- **Tracing paper and pencil**
- **Stiff paper or cardboard**
- **Scissors for paper**
- **Pins**
- **Marker pen**
- **Fabric glue**
- **Needle and matching thread**
- **Small button**

Star place cards

Draw a star on paper and transfer this to stiff paper or cardboard to use as a pattern. Cut out the star from felt, embroider an initial on it, then glue to a piece of stiff folded cardboard or cartridge paper.

1 Cut a strip 7cm/2¾in wide from each square of coloured felt.

2 To make a template for the appliquéd decoration, trace the template from the back of the book and transfer it on to cardboard or stiff paper. Cut out. Place the template on one of the strips of felt and trace around the pattern using a pen, then cut out the shape carefully, just inside the outline, using very sharp scissors.

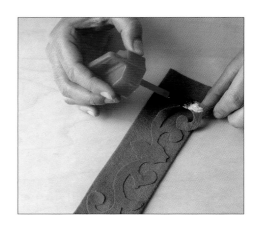

3 Using fabric glue, stick the fretwork pattern to the napkin ring or hand-sew it using small running stitches. Turn under and glue a 1cm/½in hem along each long side of the strip to give it a little stiffness. Stitch a small button to one end and cut a hole at the other end the same distance from each side for fastening.

Bead napkin ring

This elaborate-looking ring is easy to make. You need small beads for the sides and large ones for the "rungs", but they don't need to match: a variety of beads makes the finished ring more attractive.

MATERIALS

For each napkin ring:

- **Strong beading thread**
- **Scissors**
- **2 long, fine beading needles**
- **Large glass beads of approximately the same length, but varying in width and design**
- **Smaller glass beads, in two contrasting colours and slightly different sizes**

1 Cut a length of strong thread and thread a needle on to each end. Position one large bead in the centre of the thread. Add three small beads to each side of the large bead.

2 Add a large bead to one side, then pass the other needle through it in the opposite direction. Pull both threads taut. Thread three small beads on to each needle.

3 Repeat until the chain of beads is long enough to fit comfortably around a napkin. Complete by threading both needle ends back through the first bead. Knot the ends of the thread securely, thread back through a few beads and trim.

Ethnic napkin ring

Interesting beads can be knotted on to a leather thong to make a highly effective napkin ring.

MATERIALS

For each napkin ring:

- **30cm/12in tanned leather thong**
- **Selection of wooden and seed beads**

1 Make a knot about 5cm/2in from one end of the thong. Thread on a few beads of varying sizes, then tie another knot. Tie a third knot a short distance from the second knot. Add a few more beads, then tie another knot.

2 Continue threading on beads until you reach 5cm/2in from the other end of the thong. Tie the final knot. Loop the thong twice around the napkin.

Filigree beading

This delightful, intricate-looking beaded napkin ring is surprisingly robust. Made from glass embroidery beads and threaded on to silvery galvanized wire, it has a sparkle that is reminiscent of diamanté. A set of these sparkling rings would be the perfect accessory for a romantic table setting.

MATERIALS

For each napkin ring:

- **Galvanized wire or beading wire**
- **Scissors or wire cutters**
- **Pliers**
- **Glass embroidery beads**

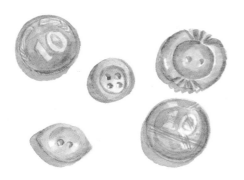

1 Cut a long length of galvanized or beading wire. Use pliers to bend one end into a small loop to stop the beads from slipping off. Thread the beads on to the whole length of the wire, then bend the other end to secure them.

2 Fashion the beaded wire into a flower shape and secure the "petals" by looping the wire around the centre. With the remaining length of the beaded wire make a ring to go around the napkin and twist the end behind the flower to secure.

OTHER CREATIVE WAYS WITH BEADS

Beaded initial

Thread short lengths of galvanized or beading wire with beads and bend them into curly letters, joining with fine wire where necessary. Tie to a napkin using fine silver cord.

Snowflake

If you don't have the time to thread the beads yourself, look out for shop-bought examples of beadwork, like this snowflake, and thread them on to fine silver cord to tie around napkins.

Punched-metal napkin ring

Modelling aluminium foil, which is available in rolls from specialist art suppliers, is strong yet easy to cut and handle. Here, it is transformed into a smart napkin ring embossed with a heart motif. A strong packaging tube makes a perfect mould for the ring, keeping it in shape while the design is punched.

MATERIALS

For each napkin ring:

- **Strip of modelling aluminium foil, 15 x 6cm/6 x 2½in**
- **Scissors**
- **Packaging tube**
- **Masking tape**
- **Pencil and paper**
- **Pin or bodkin**
- **Silver-coloured adhesive tape**

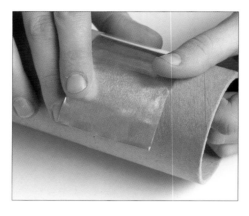

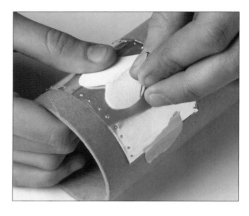

1 Fold under a 5mm/¼in hem along each long edge of the foil strip then wrap it around a strong packaging tube and secure the ends with masking tape.

2 Prick evenly spaced holes along each edge. Make a paper template for the heart motif and prick holes all round it. Join the ends of the ring with tape.

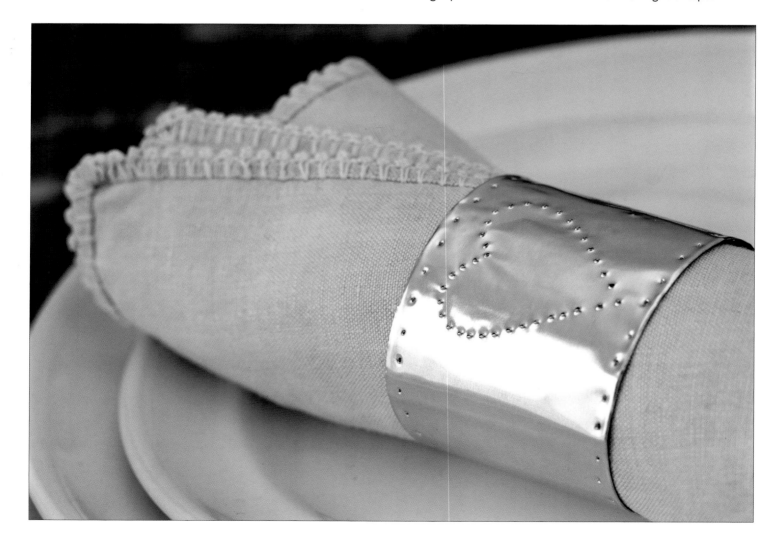

Silver service

Silvery stainless steel brings a stylish glint to contemporary table settings. This unusual and original napkin ring is a perfect match for the clean lines of modern cutlery, but is made of nothing more sophisticated than a handful of safety pins, cleverly threaded on to shirring elastic.

MATERIALS

For each napkin ring:

- **Shirring elastic**
- **30–40 stainless steel safety pins of uniform size**

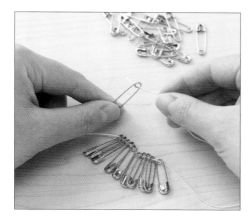

1 Tie one end of a length of shirring elastic to the ring at the bottom of one of the safety pins. Thread on the rest of the safety pins. When you get to the end, undo the original knot and tie the ends of the elastic together in a reef knot. Shuffle the pins along to hide the knot.

2 Now repeat the process with a new length of elastic, threading it through the other end of the pins to complete the napkin ring.

A touch of gold

Gold decoration on pure white china makes a glorious combination and lends an air of celebration to any occasion. Use water-based gouache paint, if you prefer to restore the napkin rings to their pure white form after the occasion, or gold ceramic paint for a more permanent, washable result.

MATERIALS

For each napkin ring:

- **2 small white elastic bands**
- **White china napkin ring**
- **Cotton buds (swabs)**
- **Gold gouache or gold ceramic paint**
- **Fine artist's paintbrush (optional)**

1 To create perfect gold circles, put two elastic bands around the napkin ring. Once they are correctly aligned, use a cotton bud (swab) to paint a line of gold spots between them. An easy way to make sure the gold spots are evenly spaced is to use clock positions as a guide. First of all, paint the 12 o'clock position, then 6, then 3, then 9, then fill in with either one or two spots in between.

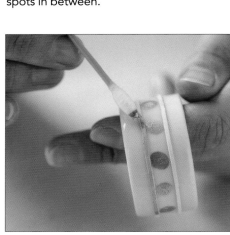

2 Once the spots are dry, touch in the elastic bands with the gold paint, using another cotton bud (swab) or a very fine artist's paintbrush.

Daisy napkin ring

The stout cardboard tubes that support rolls of furnishing fabric are an ideal size for making napkin rings, and one tube will make dozens of rings. It's possible to use thinner cardboard tubing for these painted rings, but you will need to apply more layers of papier mâché to make them rigid.

MATERIALS

For each napkin ring:

- **Heavy-duty cardboard tube**
- **Hacksaw**
- **Scissors**
- **Newspaper**
- **PVA (white) glue**
- **Mixing bowl**
- **Fine sandpaper**
- **White emulsion (latex) paint**
- **Paintbrush**
- **Water-soluble coloured pencils**
- **Gold marker pen**
- **Acrylic spray varnish**

1 Using a hacksaw, cut a 5cm/2in section of tube. Trim and tidy the edges if necessary, using scissors.

2 Tear a sheet of newspaper into narrow strips and soak in diluted PVA (white) glue. Cover the rings inside and out in two layers of papier-mâché. Leave to dry.

3 Rub the surface and edges down lightly with fine sandpaper, then paint with two coats of white emulsion (latex) paint, leaving it to dry between coats. Decorate with water-soluble coloured pencils, and edge with a gold marker pen.

4 Spray the napkin ring inside and out with a coat of acrylic varnish. Leave to dry.

Templates

Trace the templates and enlarge them to the desired size. Cut out the tracing and draw around it on to thin cardboard. Cut out carefully and accurately to create a template. When drawing around a template on to fabric use a water- or air-soluble marker pen.

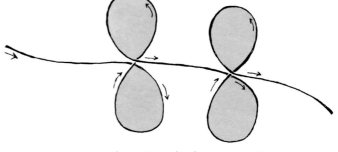

Above *Couched organza p60*

Above *Fretwork-style felt p86*

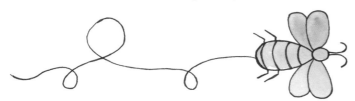

Above *Hand-painted motif p65*

Above *Cupid p61*

Above *Painted "cross-stitch" napkin p71*

Above *Painted "cross-stitch" napkin p71*

Above *Lemon slice napkin p63*

Above *Cross-stitch heart p66*
Punched-metal napkin ring p90

a b c d e f g h i j k l m
n o p q r s t u v w x y z

Above *Monograms p65*

Stitches

The stitches illustrated below are all used in the projects within the Making and Decorating Napkins chapter.

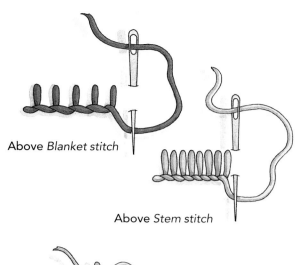

Above *Blanket stitch*

Above *Stem stitch*

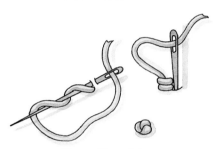

Above *Satin stitch*

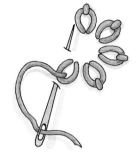

Above *Chain stitch*

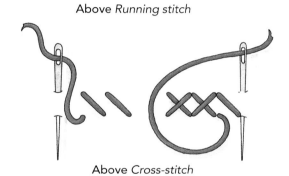

Above *Running stitch*

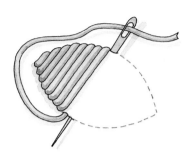

Above *French knot*

Above *Stem stitch*

Above *Cross-stitch*

Above *Fly stitch*

Above *Couching*

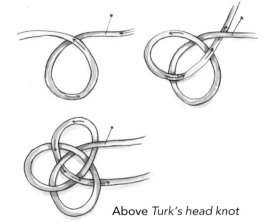

Above *Turk's head knot*

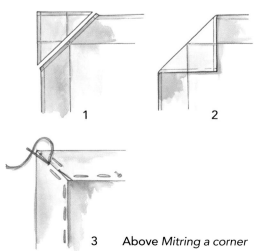

1

2

3   Above *Mitring a corner*

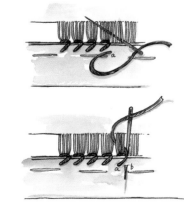

Above *Drawn-thread work*

Above *Slip stitch*

Index